Pure Reason

Practical R...

by Abbott

Hugh and Mary Ghormley

Petunia Parsonage

Des Moines   1924.

A STUDY OF KANT

CAMBRIDGE UNIVERSITY PRESS

C. F. CLAY, Manager

LONDON : FETTER LANE, E.C. 4

NEW YORK : THE MACMILLAN CO.
BOMBAY
CALCUTTA } MACMILLAN AND CO., Ltd.
MADRAS
TORONTO : THE MACMILLAN CO. OF
CANADA, Ltd.
TOKYO:MARUZEN-KABUSHIKI-KAISHA

A STUDY OF KANT

BY

JAMES WARD

FELLOW OF THE BRITISH ACADEMY
CORRESPONDENT OF THE FRENCH INSTITUTE
MEMBER OF THE ROYAL SOCIETY OF DENMARK

CAMBRIDGE
AT THE UNIVERSITY PRESS
1922

PRINTED IN GREAT BRITAIN

PREFACE

I HAVE called this little book 'a study' because it consists of a selection from notes made as a preliminary to something more systematic, which however now at my time of life is never likely to appear. I have decided to publish them—not without misgiving—in the hope that they may be of some use to students younger than myself. But I might not have got even this far, had I not been invited by the British Academy to deliver this year the annual *Henriette Hertz Lecture on a Master Mind*, and selected Immanuel Kant as my man.

The edition of Kant's works which I have used is that of Hartenstein in eight volumes, Leipsic, 1867–8. But the *Critique of Pure Reason* I have quoted according to the original paging of the first and second editions, one or both, denoting the former as A, the latter as B in accordance with present practice. The *Prolegomena*, too, I have quoted in the same way, using Benno Erdmann's edition (where the original paging is given).

I have to thank my friend, Professor G. Dawes Hicks, whose wide knowledge of Kant and extensive Kantian Library have been most generously placed at my disposal. He has helped me in many a difficulty and read through the typescript of this book. And I can never repay him.

JAMES WARD.

Oct. 31, 1922.

CONTENTS

Contents

A STUDY OF KANT

§ 1. *The Man: his Nature and Nurture*

On a broad survey of the history of Modern Philosophy it may safely be said that the lonely philosopher of Königsberg occupies the central place. The most striking features of this philosophy at the outset were its two extremes—the one eventually described by Kant himself as rationalism, the other as empiricism[1]. Descartes inaugurated the first by his *Discourse on Method* and Locke the second by his 'new way of ideas.' In Kant's 'Critical Philosophy' both the 'pure reason' of the former and 'the matters of fact' of the latter find a meeting place. From him again the diverging systems of Fichte and his Absolutist successors on the one hand, the Individualism of Herbart and the Pantheism of Schopenhauer on the other alike take their rise[2]. True, these aberrant systems did not flourish for long: some fifty years after his death the cry went forth: "We must go back to Kant[3]." The so-called Neo-Kantian movement which then began, has increased steadily and continuously ever since. No philosophers, not even Plato or Aristotle, can claim such a volume of literature, expository, philological, and polemical, as that which relates to

[1] So described, it is important to remark, only after he had himself occupied and outgrown both.

[2] Cf. J. E. Erdmann, *Die Entwicklung der deutschen Speculation seit Kant*, Erster Th. 1848, p. 24, Letzter Th. 1853, pp. 850 f.

[3] Cf. R. Haym, *Hegel u. seine Zeit*, 1857, p. 468; O. Liebmann, *Kant und die Epigonen*, 1865.

Kant. The Berlin Academy is at this moment engaged in publishing every scrap of his manuscripts that systematic search can discover; and what was said some fifty years ago—"Articles about Kant are springing up like mushrooms on every side"—is still true to-day.

Let us try first to put together from the scanty sources available a brief sketch of the nature and nurture of the man himself as a preliminary to the attempt to trace his philosophical development, to estimate what he ultimately accomplished, and understand wherein he failed.

Physically Kant was a small thin man, 'hardly more than five feet in height' and 'evanescent as a shadow.' He had a narrow sunken chest which by cramping the free movement both of the heart and lungs almost drove him in earlier years, as he has said himself, 'to feel weary of life' (*bis an den Ueberdruss der Lebensgrenzte*). But he relates how in the course of years, though the physical oppression was beyond his control, he succeeded—by resolutely diverting his attention from its effects—in preventing it entirely from disturbing his mental life[1]. But with this frail and stooping body there went an arresting physiognomy— a massive forehead, a shapely nose, and a mouth at once firm and mobile, testifying to the power of mind over body, to dispel its vapours with their brooding darkness and to irradiate life's daily round with cheerfulness and confidence—a power, and therefore a duty, which Kant both preached and practised. But Kant's most striking feature—noted by everybody—were his large, sparkling yet penetrating blue eyes—betokening kindliness and

---

[1] Cf. the interesting piece of autobiography—where one would least expect to find it—in *Der Streit der Facultäten*, 1798, Hartenstein's *Sämmtl. Werke*, VII. p. 416.

sprightly wit as well as alertness and critical acumen. No wonder then, that in spite of his consuming zeal for philosophy, he every day found time for social relaxation. It was his invariable rule to dine in company, generally with guests of his own choosing, rarely his own colleagues but for the most part 'civil servants, physicians, clergymen and enlightened merchants' among these especially two Englishmen—Green and Motherby. He made a point too of having 'a due balance of *young* men, frequently of *very* young men, students of the University, in order to impart gaiety and juvenile playfulness to the conversation[1].' On these occasions Kant was extraordinarily entertaining, abounding in information gathered from all branches of science and literature, combined with an exhaustless fund of anecdote. He read satirical books eagerly—*Don Quixote, Hudibras, Gulliver's Travels*—and he was himself addicted to satire of a good-natured sort. In short, his versatility and *bonhomie* were amazing. It is not surprising, then, that "this bachelor philosopher was declared by friends to be the most agreeable man they had ever met in society" or that so many found it hard to believe that this was the Kant who had written the *Critique of the Pure Reason*[2]. Of his kindness and concern for the welfare of deserving students numerous instances are on record, testifying, as Kuno Fischer puts it, to '*der Wohlwollen seines guten Herzens in der liebenwürdigsten Weise*[3].'

No doubt the integrity and trustworthiness which earned for him the title of *der ehrliche Kant* were native traits only

---

[1] Wasianski, *Immanuel Kant in seinen letzten Lebensjahren*, 1804, as rendered by De Quincey, "The last Days of Kant," *Miscellanies*, 1858.

[2] Stuckenberg, *The Life of Immanuel Kant*, 1882, p. 181.

[3] *Immanuel Kant*, 4te Aufl. 1898, i. pp. 118 f.

needing to be fostered; yet we can as little doubt that the
awe Kant felt in the presence of conscience with its categorical imperative was largely due to the influences exerted
both by his home life and his life at school. His mother,
his father and F. A. Schultz, who was their pastor as well
as head of the gymnasium to which in his eighth year
Kant was sent, were all 'Pietists[1].' Much there was in the
Puritanic austerity and gloomy asceticism of these Pietists
which was little better than a strait-jacket to the alert and
agile intellect of the youthful Kant; yet, all this notwithstanding, the moral influence of his parents and of Schultz,
whom he esteemed 'one of the first and most excellent of
men,' was lasting and profound. Long after he had lost
all sympathy with Pietism as such, Kant still recognised
that, as he said, "it contained the root of the matter. Let
men say of it what they will," he continued, "it suffices
that those who sincerely adopted it...possessed the highest
good which man can enjoy—that repose, that cheerfulness, that inward peace which no passions could disturb.
No want and no persecution could dishearten them; no
contention could excite them to anger or to enmity. In a
word, even the mere onlooker was involuntarily compelled
to respect[2]." Perhaps "it is not too much to say," as a
recent biographer writes, "that the world is indebted to
Pietism for saving from obscurity the greatest of modern
metaphysicians[3]." At any rate it seems 'not too much to
say' that Pietism it was which determined his main aim:

[1] Pietism was the name for an important 'revival' movement in the
Lutheran church which began some fifty years before Kant's birth. It
is often compared with the 'Methodist' movement in our established
church.
[2] F. T. Rink, *Ansichten aus Kant's Leben*, 1805, p. 13.
[3] Stuckenberg, *op. cit.* p. 15.

he remarked himself that "the origin of the Critical Philosophy is in Morality—responsibility for actions[1]."

There is however no evidence to shew that Kant was a born philosopher, or indeed precocious in any way. It happened that the ablest teacher in the Fridericianum, his gymnasium, was one Heydenreich; under him he acquired a solid training in the Latin language and literature, as is shewn, it is said, by the good Latin which he wrote and spoke, as well as by the many apt quotations from the Latin poets in which his works abound[2]. Before leaving the gymnasium young Kant and two of his fellow pupils were fired with the idea of becoming classical scholars, studied their favourite authors together, made common plans for the future, and agreed to latinise their names, Ruhnkenius, Cundius and Kantius. The first alone achieved the fame he dreamt of, the second like so many Germans of promise died early in penury. As to Kant,

[1] R. Reicke, *Lose Blätter*, i. 1898, p. 224. Morality was, in fact, the centre of gravity of Kant's endeavours. In dealing first with his theoretical philosophy we shall do well to remember that even here God, Freedom and Immortality were the ideas round which his thoughts revolved. What can I know? what ought I to do? and what may I hope for? were the questions that his whole life through he strove to answer. The idea of God was, as we shall see, central from the first in its speculative, though not in its practical bearings. When at length he came reluctantly to recognise the impossibility of proving the existence of God his philosophical outlook was essentially changed. After all, the limitations of knowledge made room for faith; and faith, he believed, was what the moral training of the world required. Cf. the fine concluding paragraph of the *Dream of a Ghost-seer* (1766), *Werke*, ii. pp. 380 f.; Letter to Marcus Herz (1773), viii. p. 695; Preface to the 2nd ed. of the *Critique* (1787), B. pp. xxx ff.

[2] In Kant's day and indeed long after, as Porson's well-known taunt shewed, the study of Greek in Germany was woefully neglected and Kant remained practically ignorant of it to the last. Cf. A. Ludwich, *Kant's Stellung zum Griechenthum*, as reported, *Kantstudien* (1900), iv. p. 328 f.

who passed into the University at the age of sixteen, new
and very different visions gradually opened out.

§ 2.　*His early interest in physical problems*, 1747–58

It was commonly believed that he matriculated in the
theological faculty in accordance with the wishes of his
father and Dr Schultz, who was himself professor of theology at the time. This, however, has been shewn to be a
mistake. It is, however, probable that Schultz directed his
studies, and that it was he who selected a rising young super-
numerary or *professor extraordinarius*, Martin Knutzen, a
broad-minded Pietist, to be Kant's teacher in philosophy.
The two, it is reported, soon became intimate: Knutzen
placed his extensive library at Kant's disposal and gave
him direction in his reading. In this way Kant became
acquainted with the works of Newton[1]. What Newton
called 'Natural Philosophy,' *i.e.* Physics rather than Metaphysics was in fact the field in which Kant first appeared
as an author. Ten out of the eleven articles in the first
volume of his collected works (as chronologically arranged
by Hartenstein) deal with physical problems, and all were
written between his twenty-second and his thirty-second
year. In these he broached several original hypotheses
which long years afterwards were independently verified—
the nebular hypothesis, the retardation of the earth's rota-
tion in consequence of the tides, the causes of the circula-
tion of the winds, and many more. Three points in the

---

[1] But this favourite teacher did more than influence his students to
become learned; he aimed to make them originators not mere imitators;
and thinkers instead of mere learners (Stuckenberg, *op. cit.* p. 45). This is
worthy of notice for in Kant's teaching too the same characteristic was
always conspicuous.

writings of this decennium may be mentioned which are relevant to Kant's philosophy in the stricter sense.

First, he held throughout it, in common with Newton, that objective, realistic, view of space, which Leibniz had rejected. Still, though 'objective,' space at first was not for Kant something absolute and independent of the things which it contained. On the contrary it was things, which by their interaction give rise to spatial relations[1]. Accordingly Kant conceived that spatial relations different from ours—spaces of higher dimensions, *e.g.*—might exist in worlds different from ours. Here again he anticipated a later hypothesis—that of the so-called metageometers.

Secondly he modestly but none the less sharply reprehended what he afterwards called the *ignava ratio* which led Newton to rest content with the description of nature as it is. Science, he maintained, should investigate the causes of every effect; how far the laws of nature suffice to account for nature being what it is, was then a question which science could not shirk. To refrain from such an inquiry on religious grounds was not the way to reconcile theism with science but the way to discredit it altogether. Newton's mechanical cosmology implied a mechanical cosmogony and the more the two could be expounded as one continuous whole, the more of a divine revelation this whole would be. Kant's attitude to Newton's cosmology was in fact very much the same as Darwin's just a century later to the biology of Cuvier; he refused to stop short leaving reasonable questions unanswered. So he was led to anticipate Laplace[2]; but with one important difference.

---

[1] *Gedanken von der wahren Schätzung u.s.w.* 1747, §§ 9–11.

[2] In an originally anonymous work entitled: *General History of Nature and Theory of the Heavens: an Essay concerning the Constitution and the*

The very cosmogony that supported theism for the youthful Kant in 1755 rendered theism 'an unnecessary hypothesis' for Laplace in 1795. Kant agreed with Laplace so
far as the physics went but at the same time sided with
Newton in regard to their metaphysical presupposition[1].

Thirdly, he realised in spite of his mechanical bias, that
the facts of animate nature belong to an altogether different
plane. The exactness of the mechanical scheme of nature
was such that one might say (and Descartes, in fact, did
say it): grant me matter and I will shew you how a world
shall arise therefrom. Such language, Kant made bold to
assert was less presumptuous than it would be to say, Give
me matter and I will shew you how a worm could be en-
gendered. Thus early he foreshadowed a problem to which
he only returned more than thirty years later[2].

§ 3.   *His first philosophical work:* Principiorum primorum cognitionis metaphysicae nova dilucidatio

By Knutzen, who had introduced him to the study of
Newton, Kant was also thoroughly indoctrinated in the
Leibniz-Wolffian rationalism which, though assailed and
controverted from many sides, was still in vogue. So it was
that—though he had become a disciple of Newton—Kant

mechanical Origin of the Universe treated on Newtonian principles—an
undertaking to which he was himself led by an Englishman, Thomas Wright
of Durham, with whose work, *An Original Theory or Hypothesis of the
Universe*—published in 1750—he became acquainted through a summary
which appeared in 1751 in a Hamburg journal. For a full account see
Professor Hastie's interesting book on *Kant's Cosmogony*, 1900.

[1] But Kant did not stop here either. This metaphysical presupposition
also he came at length to regard as dogmatism, that is to say as asserted on
grounds that were epistemologically defective. Cf. note 1, p. 5 above.

[2] Cf. below, p. 127.

set out on his philosophical career as a rationalist; and to rationalism—but a rationalism restricted and shorn of its metaphysical beams by empiricism—he adhered to the end. Gradually sifting out what was false and combining what seemed true in each, he elaborated the new theory of know-ledge—or new theory of experience, as it may perhaps be more truly called—which he himself called *Criticism*. This was his main occupation during the ensuing twenty-five years (1755–1781).

Rationalism has a long and varied history carrying us back to Plato and Aristotle, but its true epistemological character was veiled by a specious analogy which they adopted, one that remained current and not seriously challenged until quite modern times. I refer to what the Scholastics called the *lumen naturale*—a sort of intellectual instinct, the counterpart of the blind instinct of the brute—a natural revelation apart from experience, of the highest truth concerning God and man. By Leibniz however the metaphor was epistemologically interpreted, embodied that is to say in the two principles of contradiction and of sufficient reason. Wolff, whose mission it was to systema-tise the work of his great master, attempted to derive the second principle from the first; and accordingly defined philosophy as the science of the possible since whatever is non-contradictory is (logically) possible. For so doing he has earned and deserved the title of 'logical fanatic.' Whereas his predecessors had started from reality in some form or other, he chose to begin with possibility, what the principle of contradiction could guarantee and logic con-nect in a *catena veritatum* or science of essences. As to the *complementum possibilitatis* which constitutes actuality or existence—this was not the concern of philosophy but of history. A sufficient reason for such existence there must be, and then the second principle comes into play, which however was only an application of the first: the absolute necessity of his metaphysics yielded, he assumed, the 'hypothetical necessity' of his physics.

But here, where Wolff rushed in, Leibniz had feared to tread. For to make logical necessity sole and supreme was to accept the standpoint of Spinoza, who repudiated teleology, the cardinal doctrine of Leibniz himself, as but an *asylum ignorantiae*. But in fact Wolff's attempt to reduce the two principles to one proved an egregious failure: he only got along by smuggling empirical data into his philosophy of the possible at every turn. Thus no sooner was rationalism reduced to its outwardly most perfect form than the incoherence of its contents began to shew itself. Crusius, a Leipzig professor of philosophy and theology—a man of whom Kant always speaks with the greatest respect, was the first to put his finger on the weak spot—there all the time but made more obvious by the Wolffian logic—*viz.*, the surreptitious identification of ground or reason with cause. *Ratio sive causa* and *causari= sequi* occur in Spinoza; and the same confusion persisted throughout the Leibniz-Wolffian rationalism.

To a discussion of these principles and their connexion Kant's first metaphysical treatise was devoted[1]. One main object of it—perhaps *the* main object—seems to have been to 'overturn from its foundations' the Leibnizian doctrine of pre-established harmony and to establish in its place a *mutuum commercium* of all things on Newtonian lines, a

---

[1] *Principiorum primorum cognitionis metaphysicae nova dilucidatio*, 1755 (*Werke*, 1. pp. 367 ff.), a public dissertation required of him by statute on his admission as lecturer, and so given in Latin.

nexus implying that entity we call God by which it is sus-
tained, which is its ultimate ground (*Urgrund*). Despite his
dissent from Leibniz on this particular point, Kant in 1755
was what one might call an orthodox but progressive
Leibniz-Wolffian: hence the pains he took to find a rationalistic basis for his Newtonian cosmogony[1]. So it was that
he was led to attempt an independent formulation of epistemological first principles as rationalism conceived them.
In the course of this he accepted and emphasized the distinction between *ratio veritatis* and *ratio existentiae* or
actualitatis, which Crusius in his concern for a metaphysical
doctrine, that of 'free-will'—not, be it observed, in the
interests of a theory of knowledge—had been led to make.
Hence with the *crux metaphysicorum* as Kant afterwards
called it—the problem of cause—staring him in the face,
Crusius failed adequately to realise its epistemological
significance. Stranger still Kant himself, though his theme
was professedly epistemological, failed still more. Perhaps
this is one of the most extraordinary of the many instances
in the history of thought of what to posterity seems the
almost fatuous limitations even of great minds. For us now,
Crusius to all intents and purposes anticipated Hume's decisive attack on dogmatic metaphysics. Years later Kant in
a well-known passage freely confessed that by this "attack

---

1 In fact what one of his commentators calls '*eine durchgängige Ver-
mittlungstendenz*' was characteristic of his mind almost to the last. In his
first juvenile essay, in which his aim was to reconcile the Cartesian and the
Leibnizian definitions of what was then called force, he wrote: "We are
in a way maintaining the honour of human reason when we reconcile it
with itself in the different persons of acute thinkers and discover the truth,
which is never entirely missed by men of such thoroughness even if they
directly contradict each other" (*Gedanken von wahrer Schätzung der leben-
digen Kräfte*, § 125). Cf. Vaihinger, *Commentar zu Kant's Kritik d. r.
Vernunft*, 1. 1881, p. 58, for many other instances.

(*Angriff*) Hume struck a spark...which put an end to his own dogmatic slumber and gave an altogether new direction to his investigations in philosophy[1]." Why was this spark not struck either by Crusius, or by Kant himself who had accepted his distinction? Because the radical difference between logical determination (ground and consequence) and real determination (cause and effect) was not yet clear to either of them; and, as has been happily said, you cannot get a spark out of two soft stones. Kant in fact merely set to work to refute the dogma of Crusius concerning unmotived will; and instead of getting nearer to Hume got nearer to Spinoza. For Spinoza had spoken of *Deus sive natura* just as he had of *ratio sive causa*: for him the connexion of ideas on the one hand and the connexion of things on the other were the same: for him *causari = sequi*. And for the nonce this was so far Kant's position too.

On the whole it must be allowed that Kant did not effect much by his *Nova Dilucidatio* as he called it. He shared Leibniz's inability to decide whether the two principles, that of identity and contradiction and that of determining ground were reducible to one or not; but he saw that the Leibniz-Wolffian distinction between absolute necessity and hypothetical necessity was nonsense[2], and that to deduce an absolute reality from absolute necessity was equally nonsense[3]. He was, however, still hampered by the trammels of rationalism consequent on the confusion of essence and existence, in other words by the tendency of speculation to hypostasize its concepts. It was long before he could divest himself of these. Of the 'slight indications' of a movement towards empiricism which some

[1] *Prolegomena, u.s.w.* 1783, Preface pp. v–xiii.
[2] *Op. cit. Werke,* i. p. 381.   [3] *Op. cit.* p. 375.

commentators find in this first metaphysical treatise, Kant, as I have hinted, was probably not very conscious himself. It was not yet certain whether physics or metaphysics was to become the main concern of his life. At this stage at any rate his interest was divided between the two. This is a point we shall have to bear in mind if we are to understand his earlier works. The next eight or nine of his writings were still about physical subjects; and an interval of some seven years elapsed before he returned to philosophical questions. Then, between 1762 and 1766 he produced in quick succession a number of shorter treatises in all of which a swing towards empiricism and away from rationalism is unmistakeable.

§ 4. *Short Treatises with an empirical trend:* 1762–6

In the longest and probably the earliest of these Kant resumes the discussion of the problem which from first to last was for him of cardinal importance, *viz.*, that concerning the Being of God and his relation to the world. It is entitled, *The Only Possible Basis for the Demonstration of the Existence of God*[1]. Regarded as a metaphysical work

---

[1] *Werke*, ii. pp. 107 ff. The greater part of this work is occupied in applying this 'only basis' to strengthen and complete the *à posteriori* (physico-theological) proof of the divine existence: it leads Kant to elaborate further the argument of his *Theory of the Heavens*. This lengthy digression, coupled with some remarks in the preface and at the conclusion (cf. pp. 112 *fin.*, 205 *fin.*), makes the true interpretation of the whole more or less uncertain. But accepting the title as indicating its main interest, the second and longest of its three sections becomes mostly irrelevant; and the rest does little more than advance nearer to the logical consequences of an argument that had already appeared in the *Nova Dilucidatio* (cf. *op. cit.* i. p. 376). But the primary aim of that work too is doubtful; and no wonder, for so far—as already remarked—Kant was himself scarcely conscious of the subordination of 'natural philosophy' to the philosophy in the stricter

this whole essay is in the main thoroughly rationalistic in the Wolffian sense, and so far altogether fallacious. In fact the very 'basis' which Kant had prepared for a new ontological argument renders all such arguments nugatory in advance, as he himself at last fully allowed. The said basis itself consists of two propositions which are announced at the outset: (1) as to what existence is not, and (2) as to what it is. It is these alone that for the moment concern us. As just said, they really dispose of the old ontological argument for the being of God—and indeed of rationalistic ontology generally—root and branch. But Kant was, as yet, by no means prepared to accept all the consequences to which his empirical trend was leading him. His negative proposition—on which by the way it should be noted, Hume had already insisted—he states thus: "Existence (*Dasein*) is in no sense a predicate or determination of anything whatever—a proposition, which —paradoxical and contradictory as it may appear—is," he maintained, "nevertheless indubitably certain[1]." He condescends to give an illustration, as indeed he frequently did in his earlier works. Take the land unicorn (of heraldry) and the sea unicorn (the Narwhal of zoology): of the latter we can say, it exists; of the former, we can not. But our idea (*Vorstellung*) of this is just as definite as our idea of that. In fact, so far as logical analysis goes, the generic idea is one and the same: no *predicate* of unicorn is lacking in the one case—that of the land unicorn—that is present in the other—that of the sea unicorn—and *vice versa*. A unicorn is just a unicorn and nothing more whether we

sense—still for him embryonic—which that was helping to differentiate and articulate.

[1] *Op. cit.* p. 115.

think of it as living on land or in the sea. What, then, if it is not a difference of predication, is the difference that justifies us in speaking of the one as existing and yet prevents us from so speaking of the other? Simply that we are acquainted directly or indirectly with the *fact* of such existence in the one case and are not in the other. Strictly speaking, then, we ought not to say, a sea unicorn is an existing animal; but, conversely, to an existing sea-animal belong all the predicates which 'unicorn' connotes.

This brings us to his affirmative proposition: "Existence is the *absolute* positing (*Position*)[1] of a thing; thereby it is at the same time distinguished from any and every predicate, for predicates are never posited (*gesetzt*) except *relatively* to some other thing[2]." Only that is absolutely posited, which is *given in experience* as actual, as 'matter of fact.' On the other hand what is merely predicated, is only posited relatively, of an object that is *possible in thought*, *viz.* the 'subject' of a proposition; but thought cannot posit the actual existence of any object. This is the distinction Kant emphasized in using the term 'absolute position[3].' Predication as relative, presupposes the possibility of this as absolute. Reality again is not the *complementum possibilitatis*, as Wolff assumed, but its *conditio sine qua non*. "Accordingly," Kant announces further, as a sort of corollary to his two main propositions, that "all [real] possibility implies (*ist gegeben in*) something or other that is actual." It is from this point that he proceeds laboriously

[1] That Kant did not use this term as equivalent to Fichte's *Urposition* or creation, as some have supposed, is evident from the context.

[2] *Op. cit.* p. 117.

[3] It is what is nowadays called an existential proposition and it has involved such logicians as imagine it to fall within their province in bootless controversies. Cf. an article of the writer's, *Mind*, 1919, pp. 258 ff.

but tentatively to outline his new ontological argument. We can hardly refrain from indicating the confusions it involves, if only to shew to what an extent Kant was still entangled in the Wolffian meshes.

He distinguishes two senses of possibility—the logical, which he calls internal or absolute, and the real, which in general is only contingent, matter of fact. There is no contradiction, he says, in denying all existence; but if one were then to assert that there is anything possible, this would be a contradiction; since the possible implies the actual. Presently he goes on to speak not of denying (*Verneinung*) but of annulling (*Aufhebung, Beraubung*), and to argue as if the two ideas were the same. But logical contradiction does not annul the actual but only the impossible. It is true that one cannot deny all existence and yet affirm anything to be possible; not, however, because the two statements are logically contradictory, but because they are really incompatible; for as Kant began by shewing real possibility is not a matter of predication but of absolute position. Clearly then, the 'absolute possibility' of logic cannot precede, and as it were outflank, 'the absolute position' of reality. Therefore to argue from the possibility of anything to the existence of God, as he proceeds to do, is utterly inconsistent with the premises he has himself laid down. The obvious fact that *denying* existence itself implies existence—*nego, ergo sum*—and so is after all a contradiction, he seems to overlook altogether[1]. Further, if the old ontological argument is not valid, because no concept—and therefore not even the concept of God—involves existence, his new ontological argument, which

[1] Yet he recognised it later when stating the so-called 'cosmological argument.' Cf. A. pp. 604 = B. pp. 632.

infers the absolute necessity of this existence from the concept of anything at all, is still more glaringly invalid. Moreover, he had already in the *Nova Dilucidatio* denounced as *absonum*, the attempt to deduce absolute reality from absolute necessity. "*Existit; hoc vero de eodem et dixisse et concepisse sufficit*[1]."

Closely connected with this comparatively lengthy but incoherent performance is a much shorter but more important one published about the same time, and entitled, *An attempt to introduce the concept of negative magnitudes into philosophy*[2]. Here again it is interesting to find that it was Kant's physical studies that pointed the way to further advance. Important though this essay is, yet—like most of Kant's work—it is prolix and needlessly encumbered with details, which rather obscure than illustrate the main issue. This can be stated very simply. The use of the terms 'positive' and 'negative' and of their respective signs + and − both in formal logic and in the real sciences had been the occasion of much confusion, he remarks; and therefore he begins by making this difference clear. Opposition is implied in both cases. But in logical opposition we have two contradictory terms, one of which literally negatives the other: a subject of which both are predicated is unthinkable, is nothing. In real opposition there is no contradiction, for we are not dealing with a positive and a negative predicate but with two positive magnitudes. We *call* one 'negative' to be sure, but it is immaterial which; for all that we mean is that the two actually do or potentially

[1] *Op. cit.* I. p. 375. As to the argument here dealt with, cf. II. pp. 121 ff.
[2] The precise order of the writings of this period is uncertain; but it is also unimportant. They constitute one stage in our philosopher's development and probably were all worked up together. Cf. K. Fischer's *Im. Kant und seine Lehre*, 4te Aufl. 1898, I. p. 200.

might, conflict, though they could never concur. An east
wind and a west wind for a ship crossing the Atlantic, or
the debts and assets of the same balance sheet thus actually
neutralise each other—which implies of course that both
are equally real. In spite then of this use of the same
terminology, logical opposition and real opposition have
nothing in common.

The mistake of the rationalists in including both together as cases of 'sufficient reason' is now apparent: it
becomes even glaring when this principle is itself reduced
to that of contradiction. "You infer one proposition from
another in which it is already implied," Kant says to them;
"but what I want to know is simply this: how *because*
something is, I am to understand *something else coming or
ceasing to be*?" Assertion of the one fact does not *logically*
involve either assertion or denial of the other. On what
ground, then, is either made? Such ground cannot be that
of logical identity or contradiction. The difference between logical and real opposition is thus parallel to that of
logical and real ground; and the result of the one discussion
is applicable to the other. So you are not going now to
put me off (*abspeisen*) by words like cause and effect, force
and action, for these only beg my question. They merely
surreptitiously assume the very relations to be explained
unless they can themselves be traced back to a proposition
that is either self-evident or logically demonstrable. After
pondering over the question Kant is confident for his part
that no such proposition exists. Yet he believes he has
found a possible solution; it is, however, not a proposition but a concept. This somewhat enigmatical result he
promises 'some day to explain at length.' Meanwhile he
concludes by ironically inviting 'those who arrogate to

themselves unlimited insight to try how far they can succeed in finding an answer to his question[1].'

In the last of this series of his works *The Dreams of a Ghost-seer illustrated by the Dreams of Metaphysics* he more or less incidentally and only partially redeems his promise; for this was then not his main object. Just now, however, it is the one point that concerns us. A single condensed quotation will suffice to make it clear: "Philosophy has reached the end of its tether," Kant here says, "when it comes to relations which are fundamental (*Grundverhält-nisse*); and how anything can be a cause or possess a force (*Kraft*), it is impossible for reason to discover:...Thus the basal concepts (*Grundbegriffe*) of things as 'causes,' the concepts, *i.e.* of their 'forces or actions,' unless derived from *experience*, are entirely arbitrary and can neither be proved or disproved....Since rational grounds (*Vernunft-grunde*) are not of the smallest value in such cases...one must leave the decision to experience alone. Whether for example the vaunted power of the magnet to cure tooth-ache is as real as its known power to attract steel, only future experience can decide[2]."

So far Kant is at one with Hume, and their language is strikingly similar. "When we reason *a priori*," said Hume, "and consider merely any object or cause, as it appears to the mind, independent of all observation, it never could suggest to us, the notion of any distinct object, such as its effect; much less shew us the inseparable and inviolable connexion between them. A man must be very sagacious,

---

[1] *Werke*, II. pp. 104 ff. Kant's tone here will, I fear, be regarded as justly reprehensible. He seems to forget how long he lived himself in the glass-house at which he is now throwing stones. Still less did he foresee that he would one day patch it up and return to it.

[2] *Op. cit.* II. pp. 378 f.

who would discover by reasoning that crystal is the effect of heat, and ice of cold, without being previously acquainted with the operation of these qualities....When it is asked, *What is the nature of all our reasonings concerning matter of fact?* the proper answer seems to be, that they are founded on the relation of cause and effect. When again it is asked, *What is the foundation of all our reasonings and conclusions concerning that relation?*, it may be replied in one word EXPERIENCE[1]." And this is the concept that Kant in his *Essay on Negative Quantities* promised to explain at length. Up to this point, however, the promise, as I have said, is only partially fulfilled. For Hume continued: "But if we still carry on our sifting humour and ask, *What is the foundation of all conclusions from experience?* this implies a new question, which may be of more difficult solution and explanation." This is the question that Kant had not yet considered; and when he did he found himself here no longer in agreement with Hume.

While still occupied in distinguishing logical predication and real position, and in contrasting logical opposition and real opposition, it so happened that Kant was led to broach yet a third problem closely connected with these[2]. At the beginning of his treatise concerning the *Demonstra-*

---

[1] *Essays*, Green and Grose's ed. 1875, ii. p. 28.

[2] The occasion was a prize offered by the Berlin Academy in 1761 for the best treatise on the question 'whether metaphysical truths generally and especially the first principles of Natural Theology and Morals admit of the same evidence as mathematical; and if not, wherein their evidence consists.' Here was an opportunity of unburdening his mind, which Kant was unwilling to miss. Accordingly—almost at the last minute, so to say—he wrote what he himself describes 'as a short and hastily composed' *Inquiry concerning the Evidence of the Principles of Natural Theology and Morals* (*Werke*, ii. pp. 283 ff.), and sent in the manuscript with apologies just within the time prescribed.

tion of the Being of God and again in the essay on *Negative Magnitude* he had inveighed against the propensity to imitate the method of mathematics which had misled philosophers for so long. In this new essay—the so-called *Prize Essay*[1]—he returns to the same topic; and it is only this part of his essay which for the present concerns us. So far from admitting any similarity between the methods of mathematics and philosophy, he insists on their radical differences. The mathematician starts with definitions, precise, simple and complete, which he makes himself. The philosopher has to start, not with concepts which he has himself framed, but with such as are given to him in experience; and these are in general complex as well as confused or insufficiently determined; and many are altogether indefinable—such as space, time, existence, possibility, necessity, body, soul, God, and so on. To illustrate the difference Kant takes the concept of a trillion and the concept of freedom. About the relation of a trillion to its component units there is no dispute among mathematicians, but concerning the meaning of freedom, there is so far no agreement among philosophers. To advance, the philosopher must needs first analyze the concept he is seeking to define; afterwards comparing it with whatever marks he may have gradually abstracted in all the various cases in which it occurs; then further analyzing such marks to ensure that they do not overlap. And these marks, be it observed, are qualitative and endlessly diverse and not as in mathematics quantitative and so far essentially similar. Till this preliminary process is complete the chances are,

[1] As a matter of fact Kant's *Inquiry* was placed only second; it was published anonymously in 1764 along with the treatise by his friend Moses Mendelssohn which obtained the prize.

if he ventures to define, that he will fall into error, not that
he will light upon the truth. Thus—at the outset at any
rate—mathematics and philosophy proceed in opposite
ways. The method of mathematics is synthetic or direct
from the first, inasmuch as it provides its own definitions
and proceeds straightway to formulate its axioms, and
from these and its definitions to deduce their consequences.
The method of metaphysics, on the other hand, must be
analytic or inverse so long as its definitions and axioms
are still to seek. But will this quest ever end? To this
weighty question we must return presently.

Meanwhile there are some other differences between
mathematics and philosophy implied in this main difference, and to these Kant calls special attention. The 'universals' of mathematics are vicariously presented (*gesetzt*)
in concreto by means of figures or numerical and other
symbols, which can be manipulated according to strict and
evident rules, and the results deciphered afterwards. The
'universals' of philosophy, on the other hand, are only
indicated *in abstracto* by means of words, which—neither
singly nor in combination—can ever for a moment replace
the ideas for which they stand, as the sensible figures and
symbols (*die sinnliche Erkenntnissmittel*) of mathematics do.
Philosophy, therefore, can never avail itself of any such
computational devices as those which mathematics can
effectively employ. In mathematics again, there are but
few unanalyzable concepts—none in fact which it needs
itself to analyze; in philosophy, and especially in metaphysics, on the other hand, these are indefinitely many,
including those of mathematics, and all these ought to be
analyzed completely.

Similarly, there are in mathematics but few propositions

that can be called indemonstrable, and these are all axiomatic: in metaphysics there are innumerable such. The propositions Kant has in mind here are those that predicate the unanalyzable attributes or qualities, which are to form the basis (*Grundlage*) of the definitions it is the chief business of philosophy to discover. They are its material *data*: logic then cannot furnish these. Kant calls them fundamental truths, and compares them to axioms. Yet they are analogous to axioms only in being ultimate, and in implying the logical principles of identity and contradiction.

The mistake of the Leibniz-Wolffian rationalism in regarding those formal principles as themselves sufficient for philosophical, as distinct from historical, knowledge, Kant —following Crusius—had already exposed. But this mistake involved two others: mathematics and metaphysics, they assumed, were alike in dealing with purely conceptual knowledge, and were again alike in their methods. The refutation of the first of these errors was, so to say, staring Kant in the face, while writing as he did—of universals *in concreto* and *in abstracto*, and of symbols and words and their different manipulation—in order to refute the second. Yet for some time longer he still shared the Leibniz-Wolffian view of mathematics as dealing not with intuitions but merely with concepts.

Having shewn that the method of philosophy is analytic, Kant also maintained that "the true (*ächte*) method of metaphysics is essentially the same as the method introduced by Newton into the science of nature[1]." The two statements seem hard to reconcile. Newton entitled his great work *Principia Mathematica*, it may be said; and

[1] *Op. cit.* p. 294.

again, physics as a science rests on observation and experiment while metaphysics does not. But Kant is careful to point out that Newton only *applied* mathematics: he did not imitate its method. Again Newton was bent on ascertaining principles not on accumulating facts. This difference sufficed to entitle him to call his work *Philosophia naturalis*. For then, as even now, philosophy is a wider term than metaphysics: it includes this as a part—'the higher philosophy' Kant here calls it, as Aristotle before him had called it 'first philosophy.' Metaphysics, however, as Kant conceives it in this essay is, he says, "nothing else than a philosophy concerning the ultimate grounds of our knowledge," that is what we have come to call epistemology or theory of knowledge, rather than metaphysics or ontology, that is theory of being. But now what is the source of our knowledge of being? For Kant at this time, as for Newton, it is experience, the one source from which all real knowledge was derived, and the one field to which all knowledge was confined. Like Newton, Kant will neither indulge in hypotheses nor pretend to explain at the outset. Starting from what is first and immediately certain, he will *seek* continuously to advance, but only so fast and so far as is compatible with 'the highest possible metaphysical certainty.' But all this, it must be remembered, is only an advance towards securing the definitions without which the synthetic or constructive process of the highest philosophy can only tentatively and never effectively, begin.

Kant had, however, no difficulty in conceiving the completion of such a preliminary process; for he regarded mathematics as furnishing an instance of it. But then mathematics *begins with definitions*, and definitions too which are evident and exact: so there is really no parallel.

Will metaphysics then which has to begin upon concepts that are 'confused or imperfectly determined' ever attain to equally adequate definitions, will its preliminary quest ever end? On the whole the answer of the *Prize Essay* is that it never will. In a single passage, while allowing "that the time is yet far distant when metaphysics can proceed synthetically," he seems to entertain the idea that that time will some day come[1]. On the other hand, as already said, he cites numerous cases in which exact definition seems hopeless, and admits that in none is the finality and completeness of mathematical definitions ever attained[2].

The important point now, however, is that in assimilating what he calls Metaphysics to Newton's Natural Philosophy, Kant offers a positive, in place of a merely negative, answer to this question about method. The whole outlook is thus changed. Kant here renounces his former rationalism and ranges himself on the side of an empiricism, more or less tinged with scepticism. All attempts to ally Wolff and Newton, the two thinkers with whom his studies began, are abandoned. Like Locke and Hume he has recognised that whereas logic and mathematics deal only with 'relations of ideas,' metaphysics—like science—is concerned with relations involving existence, experience of 'matters-of-fact.' No wonder he was called the 'Prussian Hume.' What form the further development of his philosophy

[1] *Op. cit.* p. 298 *fin.*

[2] In the first *Critique*, where the arguments of the *Prize Essay* are repeated, Kant says roundly that metaphysics can lay claim to no strict definitions at all. Cf. A. p. 729 = B. p. 756. His vacillations on this point are remarkable. In the preface to his last *Critique* (*Werke*, v. p. 174 *fin.*) he declares it 'possible to achieve quite completely a system of pure philosophy bearing the title of General Metaphysics.'

would have taken, had he remained steadfast to this, his second standpoint, it might be interesting to surmise. But, as Tennyson has somewhere said, second thoughts are not best, but third; and Kant did not believe finality could be so easily attained. After all he had only renounced dogmatic metaphysics; and so, though abandoning the old problems as premature if not insoluble, he still continued to investigate the possible limits of reason—Locke's problem—but on a method of his own. He remained confident that much could be done to extend the bounds of metaphysics in this sense and to refute the scepticism of Hume.

It will be well for us, however, to pause here for a while to glance at the burning question, how far during the period we have traversed Kant had been influenced by English thinkers—a question which his commentators one and all discuss, but about which they differ more than they agree. In the course of this period we have found Kant sharply distinguishing (1) between any existential 'position' and every logical predication, (2) between the logical relation of reason and consequent and the real relation of cause and effect, (3) contrasting the methods of mathematics and philosophy, and (4) bringing 'metaphysics' into line with the philosophy of the real sciences. As regards the first two points he was anticipated by Hume, and as regards the last, both by Locke and Hume. Between Kant's exposition and that of his English predecessors there are also numerous resemblances in the language and even in the illustrations used[1]: we have already noticed

---

[1] In some cases, however, the parallel passages in Hume occur not in the *Enquiry*—with which Kant was certainly familiar—but in the *Treatise*, of which it is thought likely that he knew nothing at all. Hence it has been argued that if coincidences are all that can be asserted in these cases, there is no warrant for inferring connexion in the others. But this kind of argu-

one instance. Moreover he had himself expressed his appreciation of their work and his indebtedness to both, and in particular to Hume. Writers as diverse as Hegel and Schopenhauer have pointed out the affiliation of Kant's epistemology to Locke's[1]. Again Riehl, one of Kant's most recent and ablest commentators has said: "Locke's *Essay* is the English Critique of Pure Reason....No work of English Philosophy approaches it in completeness, not even Hume's *Treatise*...to say nothing of the fact that Hume without Locke is not to be thought of." As to Hume, he added later on: "It is no exaggeration to affirm: without Hume no Kant, without the *Enquiry concerning Human Understanding* no *Kritik der reinen Vernunft*[2]." And Kant himself has said as much, describing Hume as his "*scharfsinniger Vorgänger*[3]." That he selected a passage from Bacon's preface to the *Instauratio Magna* as his motto is surely a further sign of his affinity to English modes of thought: as Bacon regarded it as his mission to expose scholasticism, so Kant felt it was his to refute dogmatic rationalism.

ment may be used both ways and is perhaps more telling when transposed: There is certainly connexion in the case of the *Enquiry*, which Kant knew, and the more numerous and closer the parallels in the case of the *Treatise*, the greater the possibility that after all Kant was to some extent acquainted with that too. The evidence in favour of such a view, such as it is, has at any rate accumulated as time has gone on. Cf. Vaihinger, *Philosophische Monatshefte*, 1883, xix. p. 502; *Kant-Studien*, 1901, v. p. 114 *med.*; K. Groos, *Hat Kant Hume's Treatise gelesen?* ibid. pp. 177–181. *Per contra*, B. Erdmann, *Archiv f. Gesch. d. Philosophie*, 1887, i. pp. 62 ff., 216 ff. An able article, it is needless to say, but not devoid of special pleading.

[1] Hegel, *Werke*, 1832, i. p. 20; Schopenhauer, *Werke*, 1873, iii. p. 89.
[2] *Der Philosophische Kriticismus*, 1908, Bd. i, 2te Aufl. pp. 99, 308.
[3] Cf. the long passage in the preface to the *Prolegomena*, pp. 7–14.

§ 5. *The Inaugural Dissertation:* De mundi sensibilis et intelligibilis forma atque principiis, 1770

It was in 1770, four years after the publication of his *Dreams of a Ghost-seer*, that Kant's philosophy entered upon a new, the so-called 'critical,' phase. At this time also it so happened that he received two 'calls' to a full professorship from other universities, one being Erlangen and the other Jena. He was then forty-five and just entering upon the most brilliant period in his career. How much brighter and fuller that period might have been had he exchanged the dreariness and solitude of Königsberg for the sunnier climate of Jena and intercourse with men like Schiller and Goethe[1]! The easier circumstances and greater leisure that a full professorship offered would, he confessed, have decided him to break the associations of a life-time, had it not been that a vacancy in the professoriate was impending in Königsberg itself. He decided to wait for this, and was, in fact, nominated almost directly by a royal mandate of Frederick the Great to be *Professor Logicæ et Metaphysicæ Ordinarius* in his beloved Königsberg. And in spite of later and still more tempting inducements to remove[2], there he remained till the end. Five months later he delivered in Latin the *Inaugural Dissertation* by law prescribed, thereby inducting himself into his new office. He entitled it *A*

[1] Years after he complained of the lack of that 'food for the soul which in Königsberg is so entirely wanting.' *Letter to M. Herz*, Aug. 1777 (*Werke*, VIII. p. 699 *fin.*).

[2] In 1778, von Zedlitz, the Prussian Cultusminister, to whom he dedicated his first *Critique*, made repeated appeals to him to accept a professorship at Halle—then the first university in Prussia—offering him a much larger salary and the title of *Hofrat* or Privy Councillor, and besides urging the claims of a wider sphere and its opportunities. But all in vain.

Dissertation on the Form and Principles of the Sensible and the Intelligible World.

The striking thing about this work is the 'tilt-over' (*Umkippung*) gulf that seems to mark it off from Kant's precritical phase. There Kant had gradually advanced so far in the empirical direction that we find him in the *Dreams of a Ghost-seer* bidding a sad farewell to metaphysics as to a mistress he had vainly hoped to win. But here he seems again and at once to have harked back to a position—in its *results*—closely resembling that of the old dogmatic rationalism. Before attempting to ascertain or conjecture the steps which in fact led on to this change of standpoint apparently so abrupt[1], we must examine somewhat at length the leading features of the dissertation itself.

Its very title carries on the face of it a new distinction which here and hereafter was fundamental for Kant, *viz.*, that, between the *sensible and the intelligible*. For modern rationalism the difference between them was a difference merely of degree: sense-knowledge was confused and more or less obscure, thought-knowledge was clear and by analysis could be made distinct. But for the rationalism of the ancients the difference was one of kind, due to a radical difference in the faculties concerned. To this view Kant returned, adopting from Plato the term *phenomenon* to denote objects as sensibly apprehended or perceived (*wahrgenommen*), and the term *noumenon* to denote objects that

[1] 'Apparently,' one must say, for in fact throughout his empirical trend Kant never abandoned his private convictions as to the truth and value of metaphysics: nor was he ever attracted by mere empiricism. He was open-minded enough to accept what was true in it and indignant with the blind dogmatism which ignored this. Cf. the concluding section of his *Dream of a Ghost-seer* and his *Letter to Mendelssohn*, Apr. 1766 (*Werke*, VIII. p. 673). See also the excellent remarks of Adickes, *Kant-Studien*, 1897, I. pp. 13 ff.

can only be intelligibly comprehended or conceived (*begriffen*)[1].

Within each of these kinds of knowledge there was a further distinction, and again one that goes back to the ancients, that, *viz.*, between *matter* and *form*: this too now and henceforward becomes a radical feature of Kant's philosophy. In our knowledge of the sensible, the matter consists of sensations, but these are actually apprehended as temporally or spatially ordered or as both. This order we proceed reflectively to distinguish from the matter that is ordered; and so come by certain '*sensible*' presentations —so called because they *belong to sense*—which are purely formal 'intuitions' as they were afterwards called in the *Critique*. The case of intelligible knowledge is not so simple, and that for the following reason. Whereas sense is purely passive, so far as it is a mere *capacity* of the subject to receive impressions—to use the language of Locke and Hume—intelligence is a *faculty*, or subjective activity elicited by, but neither derived from nor in any way compounded out of what Kant called *sensualia*[2]; and further intelligence has a twofold use. In the first instance, it is employed in elaborating perceptual knowledge. The appearances (*apparentia*) of this perceptual knowledge are gradually organized by reflexion into what we call ex-

---

[1] Plato's main distinction was more objective than Kant's, in that it contrasted φαινόμενον with ὄν rather than with νοούμενον, whereas Kant, in the end at any rate, expressly demurred to the division of objects into phenomena and noumena, and admitted only the division of concepts into sensible and intelligible. (Cf. *Critique*, A. p. 255 = B. p. 311.) So far the distinction of αἰσθητά from νοητά would have served his turn better. However he continually vacillated between the two.

[2] The failure adequately to recognise this distinction was notoriously a defect of the English psychologists, especially of Hume and the so-called Associationists.

perience or empirical knowledge—as in physics which deals with the phenomena of external sense, and in psychology so far as it deals with those of internal sense. But however far this process may advance, however wide the generalisations we may reach, we are still within the limits of the sensible world. Even geometry, albeit an exact science, is no exception: it relates only to the sensible presentations of things *as they appear* and tells us nothing of things *as they are*. This first use of intelligence Kant calls its *usus logicus*.

But from this he distinguishes a second use of intelligence which he called the *usus realis*, and this alone is concerned with the intelligible world. Its concepts, however, are not—as the rationalists supposed—differentiated from those of the sensible world by superiority in logical clearness and distinctness. On the contrary, they are often far inferior in this respect, as the comparison of mathematics and metaphysics plainly shews; but at least their objects are real, not phenomenal. It is then by this second use of intelligence that we come to distinguish between the matter and the form of the noumenal or real world. By the 'matter' of the real world its ultimate parts are meant; and these Kant assumes can only be simple entities; for a complex part could not be ultimate and would imply form as well as matter, in other words, a failure to carry through the analysis on which we are bent. As for regarding the universe itself as a simple substance, this is merely a misuse of the word 'universe.' The form of the real world he describes as the permanent possibility of interaction or *mutuum commercium* between its constituent substances, and thus as implying *transeunt* action or causation actually manifested in diverse ways.

It is for metaphysics as *first* philosophy to set out the *principles* of this use of *pure* intellect. But to unfold these is not Kant's aim here: he contents himself by merely enumerating as examples certain of the concepts of this metaphysics and he chooses those which in fact he has just employed—possibility, existence, necessity, substance, cause. He also refers, again seemingly for illustration, to ontology and rational psychology as two of its subdivisions[1]. He expressly disclaimed any intention of giving in this *Inaugural Dissertation* even an outline of the positive contents of metaphysics as a science; for he can hardly so far have forgotten what he had so recently said, that "the time is yet far distant when metaphysics can proceed synthetically." As then—in the *Prize Essay* and even earlier —so now the thought uppermost in Kant's mind is the futility, so glaringly displayed by dogmatism, of starting right off to solve the problems of metaphysics without a preliminary investigation of knowledge. The *usus realis* of the pure understanding must, then, seek first of all to carry out this investigation indispensable to clearing the ground of the fallacies which have accumulated for want of it. This he distinguishes as its elenchtic use (§9): and he offers this dissertation as a sample of it (§8). It is part of a science which he proposed to call the Propaedeutic to Metaphysics—to dogmatic metaphysics, that is to say, or first philosophy.

[1] In fact, however, he has recognised all the chief—the so-called 'dynamical'—categories, and all the subdivisions of metaphysics, which afterwards appear in the *Critique*; for 'interaction' (*Wechselwirkung* or *commercium*) is stated to be the form of the real world, the subject of rational cosmology and of the dissertation as a whole. Cf. his §§ 8 and 9.

§ 6. *Transition from the* Dissertation *to the* Critique: 1770–81

Eleven years elapsed (1770–81) before Kant produced his next and his chief philosophical work, the *Critique of Pure Reason*: in all that long interval he published scarcely anything; in fact, nothing of philosophical importance. What little is known of his progress during all this time has had to be gathered from very various sources[1]; but all the evidence to be gleaned from these points to a continuity between the *Dissertation* and the first *Critique*, shewing the former to have been the germ out of which the latter, and even the two subsequent critiques, had gradually grown.

But there is one topic of the *Dissertation* which Kant never developed, and that is the exposition of the noumenal world which he then thought attainable by the *usus realis* of the pure understanding. For during these years of silent work he became convinced that such knowledge is beyond the ken of the mere understanding. At any rate —almost as soon as they were written—he referred to the parts of his dissertation professing to treat of this (Parts I and IV) as of no account, confessing that they were due to haste (*Eilfertigkeit*) and needed amendment[2]. He seems

[1] Of these may be enumerated, (1) his letters, especially those to Marcus Herz, who acted as 'respondent' or 'seconder' in the debate which the *Dissertation* opened, (2) a collection of loose scraps of MSS.—known as the *Lose Blätter*, edited by Reicke (1891 ff.), (3) notes scribbled in an interleaved copy of Baumgarten's *Metaphysik*, the text-book used in his lectures, and edited by B. Erdmann under the title of *Reflexionen* (1884), and (4) the *Prolegomena to every future Metaphysic* written two years after the first edition of the *Critique* as a sort of popular compendium.

[2] *Letter to Lambert*, Sept. 1770, VIII. p. 663. Nevertheless they continued to form a part of his lectures on Metaphysics to the end.

in fact to have been merely airing certain private convictions, entertained all his life long, temporarily sup-
pressed during his empirical trend and now apparently
free to rise again[1]. Already, in the last part (Part v) dealing
with method, he traces to subjective 'principles of con-
venience'—'regulative but not constitutive,' to use his
later terminology—positions which in the previous parts
he had dogmatically maintained as objective. Assuming
this hasty dogmatism abandoned, the continuity between
the *Dissertation* and the *Critique* is complete.

We can now take up the enquiry as to the intermediate
steps that may have connected the two extreme positions
separated by the shorter interval of four years (1766–70)
—the sceptical extreme of the *Dreams of a Ghost-seer* at
one end and the dogmatic extreme of this *Inaugural Dissertation* at the other—hoping thereby to establish more continuity in Kant's theoretical philosophy as a whole.

Here two steps at least are certain—both bearing on
the distinction between the sensible and the intelligible.
In 1768 Kant published a brief paper of seven pages discussing the implications in our experience of spatial
direction of what he called '*the difference of regions in
space*.' This experience he held was "an evident proof
*that absolute space is independent of the existence of material
things, and had itself—as the first ground of the possibility of
their being apprehended together (Zusammensetzung)—a
reality of its own*[2]." Comparing the right hand with the
left no difference is discernible between them so long as
we attend solely to their size, shape, etc. But in spite of

---

[1] Cf. a doctor-thesis by O. Riedel, a pupil of B. Erdmann's, *Die mono-
dologischen Bestimmungen in Kant's Lehre vom Ding an sich*, 1884.

[2] *Werke*, ii. p. 386. Kant's italics.

their perfect symmetry they cannot be brought to coincide. How is this diversity, this 'incongruence' to be explained? If space consisted only in the juxtaposition of material things—as Leibniz supposed—there would be nothing to determine a given hand as either right or left. And yet if a hand were the first thing created, it would be either a right hand or a left hand. Why? Because it would necessarily have a definite orientation. But that implies a universal space existing before it as well as beyond it. Of this space the figure of the hand as of every other thing is but a part. This one absolute space suffices not only to explain the lie (*Lage, situs*) of the several parts within these figures but the direction in which they as wholes are situated relatively to any assigned point of reference. The concept of this space cannot, then, Kant concluded, be "a mere figment of thought (*Gedankending*); yet its reality—*obvious though it is for intuition*—has its difficulties when we try to grasp it as an idea of the reason[1]." Nevertheless he held on to this reality for the time, maintaining, with Newton and against Leibniz, the objective existence of absolute space.

"The year '69," Kant noted down later, "gave me great light[2]." This year's reflexion on 'its difficulties' helped then to lead him so far to abandon Newton's position, and to adopt instead of it the position maintained in the *Inaugural Dissertation* and in the *Critique*, viz. that space, like time, is only phenomenal; in other words, has no reality in itself. The concept of space is not disclosed by the exercise of pure thought: it is due to sensible intuition as the form of external sense. The only wonder is that it took Kant so long to arrive at this solution, for throughout

---

[1] *Op. cit.* p. 391. Italics mine.
[2] *Reflexionen*, edited by B. Erdmann, 1884, ii. p. 4.

his brief paper he talked of '*intuitional* judgments': in what we first call 'here,' our body is the point of reference and the three rectangular axes through it are the directions from which we start.

But there was still a further difficulty which specially perplexed Kant at this time and this too he believed was only soluble in the same way. It arose in what he was wont to call the mathematical antinomies. Intellectually and in the abstract it is easy to think of the world as a whole and as consisting of simple parts. But when we try to represent it to ourselves in the concrete, *i.e.* by means of a definite intuition, we fail; for here time and space come in— whether we set out from the parts to reach the complete whole or from the whole to reach the simple parts. And so, since the inconceivable and the impossible (*irrepresentabile et impossibile*) were identified by dogmatic rationalism, it had to face these antinomies. What the theses affirmed of the intelligible world contradicted the antitheses derived from the sensible world, in which we attain neither to the absolute nor to the simple. So long as the distinction in kind between the sensible and the intelligible is ignored—as it was by the Leibniz-Wolffians—the scepticism these antinomies evoke could not, Kant believed, be laid. But so soon as this distinction is recognised, the spectre vanishes at once: contradictions are possible only in *pari materia*. This recognition from the intellectual side of a distinction between sense-knowledge and thought-knowledge also came to Kant—as he has himself testified —as part of the great revelation of '69[1].

---

[1] Cf. *Reflexionen, loc. cit.*, and especially the letter to Garve, written nearly thirty years later and only unearthed in 1884. *Briefe*, Berlin Acad. ed. III. p. 255.

As regards the second of the main distinctions enounced in the *Dissertation*—that between matter and form, applicable both to sensible and intelligible knowledge—it is almost certain that Kant owed this not to his own reflexions but to the influence of Leibniz's posthumously published *Nouveaux Essais*. This important work and the longest of all Leibniz's works appeared in 1765, when Kant's pre-critical period was practically over. That, during the five years subsequent to this date and prior to that of his own *Inaugural Dissertation*, Kant should have neglected to study those essays is in itself most improbable. External evidence to the contrary is not wanting[1]; while the internal evidence is too strong to be rebutted by the mere fact that Kant does not refer to the *Essais*, nor by the fact that on other points he dissented from Leibniz. It is the points of identity between them that have to be accounted for in view of the sudden and otherwise scarcely explicable swing back towards his old rationalism which we find in Kant's *Dissertation*.

We have only to recall his dejection in 1766—when convinced by his rude awakening through Hume that the metaphysics of which he was enamoured in his youth, was but a pleasant dream—to realise the wider horizon and the renewed hope that the *Nouveaux Essais* would bring. In the Introduction to the *Critique* (B. p. 1) we find Kant saying: "It is beyond a doubt that all our knowledge begins *with* experience..., but it does not therefore follow that it all arises (*entspringt*) *out of* experience." He then proceeds to shew that, *in fact*, it does not. But in 1766 he had not got beyond its first clause, embodied substantially

---

[1] Cf. Paulsen, *Entwicklungsgeschichte der Kantischen Erkenntnisstheorie*, 1875, p. 145 note.

in the scholastic *dictum, nihil est in intellectu quin prius fuerit in sensu*. Leibniz's well-known addition, *nisi intellectus ipse*[1] may well have led him to the second clause as we find it in the *Dissertation*. The resemblance as regards this distinction of matter and form is complete and extends even to the language employed; although it is one that Kant had not previously drawn. Like Leibniz he finds the asserted possibility realised not in the innate ideas controverted by Locke, but in the subjective activity or 'operations of our minds' evoked on the occasion of experience and subsequently discerned by what Locke called reflexion. Again like Leibniz, Kant speaks of these forms as *a priori, i.e.* not 'borrowed' *from (empruntées, mutuatæ)*, but, in fact, imposed upon the matter of experience; and so both universal and necessary.

There is, however, one important difference between Leibniz and Kant due to Kant's first main distinction, the distinction, that is, between sensibility and intelligibility, both of them included by Leibniz under the one term *intellectus*. On this divergence turn consequences which were decisive for Kant's system as a whole and led him to take up the extreme position we have noted as characteristic of the *Dissertation*. Sense as well as intellect has its own forms; but the first Kant was now—as we have seen—convinced pertain only to the sensible or phenomenal world. None the less they furnish the basis for mathematics. Hence arose, what we may almost call the temptation to apply to the form of the intelligible world a superficial parallel which here suggested itself. And to this temptation we have seen that Kant temporarily and partially succumbed. As there is an *a priori* science of the

1 *Nouveaux Essais*, ii. i. p. 2.

phenomenal, mathematics, so, he argued, there should be
an *a priori* science of the noumenal, metaphysics. And why
is there not? Because hitherto their utter lack of method
had doomed philosophers to a Sisyphean task. The last
part of the *Dissertation* is devoted to an exposition of the
method hitherto lacking in metaphysics.

The fundamental rule of the whole method comes to
this: the *principia domestica* of sensitive knowledge must
not be allowed to transgress their bounds and infect the
domain of pure intellect (§ 24). Cleared of such surreptitious intrusions, the *usus realis* of this would be as compe-
tent to yield us a systematic knowledge of things as they
really are, as its *usus logicus* had been systematically to
present them as they appear to us to be. But whereas in
science experience comes before method, since we start
from sensory intuition, in metaphysics—where we cannot
so start—method must come first. "For here," Kant urges,
"since the right use of reason constitutes the principles
themselves—so that solely through its nature the objects
and the axioms [of metaphysics] first become known
[*primo innotescant*]—it follows that the very exposition of
the laws of pure reason is at once the genesis of the science
and the criterion of its truth (§ 22)[1]. Kant is thus again
contemplating metaphysics at the constructive or synthetic
stage that had seemed to him so far away in 1762 (when
writing his *Prize Essay*) and that in 1766 (the date of the
Dreams of a Ghost-seer) he felt must be definitely abandoned. But this metaphysical method, it will be observed,
while excluding sensible intuition from the purely in-

---

[1] The last point reminds one of Spinoza (cf. *Ethics*, ii. xliii, Scholium)
and the whole might conceivably be regarded as an anticipation of Hegel's
Logik.

tellectual domain, has no intuition of its own. An 'intellectual intuition' is possible Kant contends, nay, is necessary; but it must be active not receptive, must be, in fact, what we try to understand as creative. Here again Kant is substantially at one with Leibniz. He is, however, forced to admit that we have only a 'symbolic knowledge' of the concepts of pure understanding or reason; since for us at any rate these concepts are devoid of all intuitive content. But what meaning are we to attach to such a phrase as 'symbolic concepts of things as they are'? Simply that it is a roundabout and covert way of saying that what things *per se* may be remains for us unknown, even though we know that they are. They are then for us just an x, and this is the negative meaning of noumenon as given in the *Critique*. There too, so far from imagining that our understanding has a positive domain of its own beyond that of sensory experience, Kant has become convinced that it has none: it is the sensible world that now sets limits to such excursions of the understanding.

How, then, we ask, was Kant, who had so effectively exposed the erroneous identification of the methods of mathematics and metaphysics, himself at last misled by the superficial parallelism between them—to wit that both are *a priori*? First, because he overlooked the fact that only concepts based on intuition imply objects: *entia rationis* are then 'empty concepts without an object[1].' Secondly, because he momentarily forgot his own doctrine that predication in the last resort implies existential 'positions.' Thus after all 'the great light' of 1769 brought Kant more problems than it solved. How these dawned upon him and how he dealt with them are the questions

[1] Cf. *Critique*, A. pp. 256 f. = B. pp. 312 f.; A. pp. 291 f. = B. pp. 347 f.

we have next to consider: they bring us to his chief work the *Critique of the Pure Reason* of 1781.

§ 7. Kritik der reinen Vernunft: 1781

(a) *The first project and its preparation*

But though his chief work, this *Critique* is out and away Kant's most slovenly performance. The minute scrutiny of the so-called *Kantphilologen* during the last thirty or forty years has placed beyond a doubt that it is the merest patchwork or mosaic of scraps, specimens of which have been collected by hundreds[1]. Out of pieces such as these, dealing, each *de novo* with one or another of the many topics that had jostled each other in his mind for at least a dozen years, Kant, in some four or five months, like a man in a hurry—to use his own expression—put together this '*weitlaüfiges Werk*,' as he called it, of over 850 pages, at first projected as a Tractate on *Method* of only a few sheets! As it stands it has been aptly compared to a geological region of highly contorted strata: with the help of some plain clues, compared to the geologist's 'characteristic fossils,' and much more or less probable conjecture—it has at length been somewhat straightened out.

The continuity between the *Dissertation* and the *Critique* we have already noted. But in fact, though printed, the Dissertation was never properly published; since Kant intended to convert it into a new work, which might be entitled *The Boundaries (Grenzen) of Sense and Under-*

---

[1] Cf. Erdmann's *Reflexionen* and Reicke's *Lose Blätter* mentioned above. These are what Max Müller would have called 'the chips from Kant's workshop': they form an invaluable 'deposit' for later commentators and we shall have presently to refer to them.

standing. In June 1771 he informed his friend Marcus
Herz, that this revised work was then practically complete. Less than a year later, however, he wrote to him
again regretting that he had found something essential
still lacking. The question, which he and many others, he
said, had overlooked was this: "On what ground does the
reference of what we call a presentation in ourselves to the
object rest?" And this, be it remarked, was one main
problem of his *Critique.* In the case of sense-presentation
there was—he then thought—no difficulty[1]; for here it is
the object (the thing as it is) that affects the subject, giving
to it certain presentations (sense-data) which it just passively
receives. With the pure concepts of the understanding,
however, the case was wholly different; for these concepts
are not the cause of the object nor is the object the cause
of them. "In the *Dissertation,*" he goes on to say, "I had
been content with [such] merely negative statements...
but this question of the relation between the two I passed
over in silence." In a 'reflexion' jotted down about this
time (1772) Kant raises the new problem still more definitely: "How does it come about that objects correspond
to what is simply a product of our mind itself alone (*sich
isolirenden*) and that these objects are bound by the laws
that we prescribe to them? That we of ourselves should
be able to make universal statements about objects, although
no experience warrants us so to do—this is a hard thing
to see into. To say that some superior being had already
wisely implanted within us such concepts and principles
means subverting philosophy altogether. [To ascertain]

[1] Although this has seemed an intractable problem from Descartes' day
to our own, a problem which Kant himself realised later on, but did not
solve. But is it soluble, and if not, is it a problem?

how a reference and connexion (*Verknüpfung*) is possible, although only one [term] of the relation (*eines von der Relation*) is given, we must inquire into the nature of knowledge as a whole[1]."

The first thing in pursuance of this inquiry, he continues in the letter to Herz, was to seek to resolve all the concepts of pure reason into classes of categories, not in the haphazard fashion of Aristotle, but by means of a few fundamental principles. He began in a very tentative fashion[1] by just reflecting; for the understanding, he observed, was the faculty of reflecting, and the categories, simply abstract concepts of reflexion[2]. Accordingly, he makes frequent mention of operations such as comparing, connecting, relating, and of the resulting concepts—identity and diversity, agreement and opposition, matter and form, etc. In the *Critique* he sharply distinguished these as merely 'concepts of reflexion' from categories as pure concepts of the understanding. Of the latter he especially mentioned Substance, Cause and Interaction along with many others—*e.g.* Position (*Setzung*), Quidditas, Number, Infinity, Action and Passion—afterwards dropped as categories and dealt with in other ways[3].

At length the category of Relation takes the lead. Kant calls it the supreme among all categories and speaks of reason as containing nothing but relations: so far he was more or less in line with Locke and Hume[4]. He further

---

[1] *Letter to M. Herz*, 21 Feb. 1772 (*Werke*, VIII. pp. 688 ff.); *Reflexionen*, II. no. 925, pp. 259 f. This then was one and indeed the chief of the problems just now referred to as the outcome of the *Dissertation*.

[2] Cf. his account of the process, 'Analysis of the Concepts,' A. pp. 65 f. = B. pp. 90 f.

[3] For his longest and most miscellaneous list, see no. 513, *Reflexionen*, II. p. 160.

[4] Cf. Locke, *Essay* IV, 1. p. 5; Hume, *Treatise*, bk. 1, pt i. § 5.

refs this supreme category to the unity of consciousness "since unity is strictly concerned only with (*betrifft eigentlich nur*) relation." From relation to judgment was an obvious step, and he continues: "This (*i.e.* relation) then makes the content of any judgment as such, and can be thought alone [as] a priori *definite*[1]." He expressed this last point later with more precision: "The unity of the consciousness of the manifold in the presentation of any object at all is the judgment. The presentation of any object at all, so far as it is made definite in respect of this objective unity of consciousness (logical unity) is [a] category[2]." So at last Kant was confident that he had found a clue to a satisfactory classification and an exhaustive enumeration of all the pure concepts of the understanding which the projected revision of the *Dissertation* had led him to seek. Here at last was a single principle in place of the few he had begun to look for, "an operation of the understanding," which, as he said, included all the rest: it consisted in judging. This unquestionably was an important step. The work of the logicians—apart from a few defects—there ready to his hand, would now enable him to exhibit a complete table of the pure functions of the understanding, or categories (to use the old term), "on which beyond a doubt our entire knowledge of things by means of the understanding can rest[3]."

But Kant had still to correct the 'few defects' of the existing formal logic in order to make his clue to the categories complete. In point of fact his clue proved to be a veritable mare's nest—the most disastrous 'discovery' he ever made. His whole procedure, indeed, was more or less

[1] Cf. *Reflexionen*, no. 596, *op. cit.* p. 183.
[2] *Reflexionen*, ii. no. 600, p. 184.   [3] *Prolegomena*, § 39.

a tampering with facts. What one of his contemporaries called his 'evil demon'—being 'too clever by half,' as we say—his unbridled acumen, lured him into fabricating what he professed to find. As his latest commentator has truly remarked: "his exposition [of the forms of judgment] is throughout controlled by foreknowledge of the particular categories which he desires to *discover*[1]." A coincidence obtained by additions on the one side and omissions on the other could neither guarantee completeness nor reveal a principle; and indeed it is very doubtful if either Kant's table of judgments or his table of categories ever found unqualified acceptance anywhere outside his own orthodox school. At least it is certain that the symmetry he supposed he had discovered, has been shewn to be 'riddled with contradictions[2].' Nevertheless Kant rated his newly discovered parallelism so highly that he plotted out his entire theory of knowledge on the lines of the old formal logic.

He was led, however, to make a distinction of cardinal importance between the two, between the old pure or formal logic and what he now called transcendental logic.

[1] Professor Norman Smith, *A Commentary to Kant's Critique, etc.* 1918, p. 193. Cf. also Hauck, "Die Entstehung der Kantischen Urtheilstafel," *Kant Studien*, 1905, xi. p. 207.

[2] The characteristic of Kant's mind here so conspicuously displayed can hardly be passed over unnoticed. Whether a feeling for order (*Ordnungsinn*) that amounted to pedantry was natural to him from the first—as Kuno Fischer supposes—or not, it had at all events become at length a second nature, mainly through the early and thorough indoctrination into the Wolffian philosophy he received from Knutzen. Kant's ideal of theoretical philosophy was of a something static, a completed structure to be analyzed, not a something dynamic, a living whole, the life of which was to be understood. Thus he talks much of the 'architectonic of pure reason,' but treated its teleology as at best but a stepchild, declining to recognise the category of end (*Zweck*) here at all. Cf. an interesting brochure by E. Adickes, *Kant's Systematik u.s.w.* 1897.

This distinction turns on the difference between form and function. The 'forms of thought as thought' with which pure logic is concerned are the products of thinking, reflectively *emptied of their content*. The functions of thinking, on the other hand, cannot be thus emptied: as actions (*Handlungen*) they must obviously deal with something. It is these pure spontaneous functions of understanding then, that are the subject-matter of transcendental logic. Obviously they are presupposed in the empty forms which the old logic reflectively dissects when the living process of thought is ended. It was just this fact, we may note by the way, which led him to look to these forms of thought— its anatomy, so to say—as the clue to its vital functions still deeply 'hidden in the depth of the soul.' Even so, once he had an inkling of the essential difference between the two, it is surprising to find Kant still setting such store by the old logic. Now, however—and thanks largely to Kant himself—it is widely recognised that, in the sense in which transcendental logic is logic, formal logic is not logic at all[1]. Unhappily, however, Kant had not the courage of his convictions and is continually reverting to the standpoint and terminology of formal logic[2].

[1] Its resting place seems likely to be that recently assigned to it, *viz.* in mathematics, as a special, or non-numerical algebra, commonly called 'symbolic logic'; in other words it is essentially computation, as Hobbes called it, and essentially not thinking.

[2] Notably in the Schematism of the Categories, a specimen of needless architectonic which we can safely ignore. This, however, is a detail that cannot be briefly disposed of. Cf. Riehl, *Der Philosophische Kriticismus*, 2te Aufl. 1906, pp. 532 ff.; Professor Norman Smith's *Commentary*, 1918, pp. 334 ff.

§ 8. (b) *The cardinal problem:* the transcendental
'Deduction' of the Categories

Nevertheless there is a good deal of evidence—besides
that discernible in this miscalled 'metaphysical deduction'
of the categories which we have just considered—tending
to shew that Kant was independently elaborating his cardinal doctrine concerning them, what he called their
'transcendental deduction.' "Jurists," he begins, "distinguish in every lawsuit...the question of right (*quid juris*)
from the question of fact (*quid facti*), and in demanding
proof of both they call the former, the *deduction*." It is in
this technical sense peculiar to law that Kant here uses
the term. The main question to be decided is *Quid juris?*
In other words, the question of justification (*Rechtmässig-
keit*) or validity: What warrant is there for the application
of these categories to experience, if—as Kant and rationalism generally assumed—they are essentially independent
of it? Here then we find Kant still engaged with the very
question which he had propounded at the outset in the
famous letter to Herz; but without waiting to ascertain
and classify all the categories first. The justification sought
is one which will apply alike to all categories, is concerned
with them collectively not severally; and so, save for illustration, none are specially mentioned; then almost in-
variably the category of cause. The notion of a single
common ground is here evident from the beginning; but
it is a ground which primarily implies a unity not of form
but of function. The inquiry, as he says in his preface,
has two sides. These, however, he failed clearly to distinguish; for, in fact, they are not separable: he called
them respectively the subjective and the objective de-

duction. The former was an excursion into psychology dealing with the preliminary question (*quid facti?*) rather than a 'deduction' in the legal sense. As to the value of this Kant had serious misgivings; in any case, though he regarded it as very important, it was not—he comforted himself by saying—essential to the main question: *quid juris?* But even in his exposition of this, the objective deduction, there is still a good deal of psychology and that none of the best; though Kant has been hailed as the great 'psychologist of the pure reason.'

He begins by referring to Locke as the 'celebrated man' whom we have to thank for first opening up the way; but then Locke, he remarks, never got beyond the *quaestio facti* of the subjective deduction: he only 'explained the *possession*[1].' This seems an unfortunate analogy. There are many kinds of legal right, but if only the right to possession were in question, to prove production should suffice: what I have made by myself and of my own is surely mine. All that it is needful to shew in that case would be that the property in question was spontaneously self-produced. Proof of the fact would then be proof of the right; and this Kant also in the first instance was at pains to shew. Locke, however, had already shewn this when he described complex ideas as those which the mind 'frames for itself' out of the simple ideas impressed upon it[2]; though of course Locke had no clear prevision of all that this spontaneous activity of thinking implied. That he had not, is sufficiently clear from his definition of knowledge as the

[1] According to an interesting passage in the preface (A. p. iii) he seemed rather 'once for all to have explained it away.'

[2] Cf. *Essay II*, ch. xii, and Riehl, *Kriticismus*, 2te Aufl. 1908, pp. 50 f. Cf. also an excellent article by Drobisch, "Ueber Locke, den Vorläufer Kant's," *Zeitschrift f. exacte Philos.* 1862, ii. pp. 1–32.

perception of the agreement or disagreement of any of our ideas. This recalls Kant's distinction between formal and transcendental logic. He complained that the explication of a judgment as the idea of *a relation between two concepts*, in vogue among logicians, failed to throw any light on the source of the *relation* itself[1]. Locke's definition of knowledge has the same defect. Knowledge through categories is not a case of simply *perceiving* the relations they imply. In the fourth book of his *Essay* Locke had forgotten a remark he had made concerning these ideas of relation in the second—that were we attentively to consider them they might 'lead us further than at first perhaps we could have imagined[2].' It may suffice for formal logic to say that a judgment can be enunciated as a proposition relating two or more terms or subordinate propositions. But transcendental logic calls for more.

Relations imply 'a concept of a higher order' than their terms. These may go back to the formless 'manifold,' the raw material of knowledge which is supposed to be passively received; but the concept of their connexion implies a unity, not the merely formal unity which is one of the categories, but a 'qualitative unity'—to use Kant's phrase —that is common to all categories. This connecting or functional unity is due to a spontaneous act, not to a merely accidental association. This act is what is meant by apperceptive synthesis. It is not enough for knowledge that its data should be strung together as occurrences (*Erlebnisse*) and so perceived in a single sentient consciousness. Only when they are, in thought, brought together in the 'apperception' of a subject *aware of its own unity*, can they be said to be effectively synthesized. Only then do

---

[1] B. § 19.   [2] *Essay II*, xii. § 8.

they form 'an object' for such self-conscious subject. Thus
the synthesis which produces a unity implies the unity of
the process whereby it is produced; *viz.* the qualitative
unity which Kant called the 'original synthetic unity of
apperception.' Thus and only thus, by our own activity
do we advance beyond the stage of mere *Erlebnisse* (as
presumably he would now say)—*Leibniz's consécutions des
bêtes*—and acquire for ourselves or come into possession
of, a connected Experience, more or less systematized
knowledge. Hence this synthetic unity, implied in saying
'*I think*,' Kant dignified with the title, *Transcendental
Unity*, the supreme principle of all understanding[1]; and
so he characterized his philosophy itself as *Transcendental
Philosophy*.

But the simple fact of possession was not the main count
in Kant's claim. He begins indeed by remarking that this
experience which we frame for ourselves is a very 'mixed
tissue.' There are many concepts for which experience
affords a sufficient title; there are some, such as 'fate' or
'fortune' in common vogue and generally tolerated, which
are mere usurpers of a status to which they have no title
at all; and there are 'a few[2]'—to wit the categories—
claiming—or rather, proclaiming—an *a priori* authority
entirely independent of experience. This is what has now
to be 'deduced,' *i.e.* justified; and so we come to the objective deduction. We come too upon a new legal analogy,
that of a *de facto* legislation and an appeal to—or a mandate
from—some court of higher authority. Experience, to
which alone Locke and Hume appealed, afforded no war-

1 *Critique*, B. §§ 15–17, pp. 129 ff.
2 This casual reference shews how little Kant is here concerned with the
metaphysical deduction.

rant for the two chief categories—substance and cause, and according to Kant, as we here see, could afford none. But to appeal to Reason, which seems the only alternative, would that not be to make the defendant in the suit also the judge?—a defendant too, as Kant proceeds in the end to shew, liable to "sophistications from which even the wisest men cannot escape[1]"! Circular reasoning, or worse —complete scepticism—seems then unavoidable. The only way to save the situation is to compare it to an appeal from Philip drunk, to Philip sober—a *critique* of reason by reason itself[2]. To understand how on these lines Kant sought to solve this 'arduous problem' we must follow his exposition a stage or two further.

First, Kant finds it needful to point out more explicitly what so far has been only implied, *viz*. that the unity of apperception entails the objective unity, in which experience at the thought-level begins; for it is through it "that all the manifold given in an intuition is unified in some concept of the object[3]." But, unfortunately, his use of the term 'object' is extremely lax[4]. He refers to the thing *per se* as an object; but as we can only think it, not know it, he distinguishes it as a *noumenon*. He also applies the term object proleptically to the 'manifold of intuition' itself; although this is *not yet* a '*determined* object,' but only what he calls the empirical object of intuition, an appearance (*Erscheinung*) or *phenomenon*. But here again his terminology is loose; for he still applies this same term phenomenon

---

[1] Cf. A. p. 339 = B. p. 397.
[2] Cf. A. pref. pp. v f., B. pref. p. xv.
[3] B. § 18.
[4] This led to a long controversy between Kant and J. S. Beck, which perhaps is now only of historical interest. Cf. Vaihinger, *Commentar*, II. 4 f.

to this inchoate object after it *is* determined as a synthesized unity; and this he does to distinguish it from the
noumenal object[1]. Secondly, if we now leave aside the
contents of any given manifold of intuition, and synthesize
only their (spatial and temporal) forms, we have what
Kant presently calls 'schematized' categories. Some content a concept must have, or it would be empty; for there
can be no handling (*Handlung*) of nothing; and some unity
the intuition must have, for otherwise it would still remain
blind or undetermined. Experience, then, as more than
sentient *Erlebnisse*, implies not only the immediate synthesis of the manifold of sense-data in intuition, but also
the further mediate or relating synthesis of thought. Both
alike are due to the subject's activity at different levels,
that of the immediate synthesis of the sensory manifold
in perception, and that of the mediate synthesis of percepts
in understanding[2]. Again both alike—so far as their forms
are concerned—are entirely independent of experience—
in the sense of what is given—and yet are the sole and
sufficient condition of experience so far as it is *a priori*.
Here again, *more suo*, Kant uses the term experience in

[1] Having seven terms at his disposal when writing in German for
philosophers, *viz*. Gegenstund, Object, Ding, Sache, Erscheinung, Phae-
nomenon, Noumenon, Kant might easily have been more precise, if only
he had thought it worth while. But there is yet a further obscurity in Kant's
exposition, which even so would not be met, *viz*. the failure steadily to
distinguish between the psychologically and the epistemologically objective.
The former is often called subjective as being the peculium of the individual
experient, and the latter alone objective as common to experience in general.
Such failure on Kant's part involved him in a faulty and ambiguous
orientation, which Professor Norman Smith has affectively signalised as a
vacillation between subjectivism and phenomenalism. Cf. also Dr G.
Dawes Hicks, *Die Begriffe Phänomen und Noumenon bei Kant*, 1897,
pp. 138 ff.
[2] Cf. B. § 17 *init.*

two senses. However, it is only with the latter meaning that he is here concerned. This is all that he thinks he has to justify.

But though the things *per se* which transcend our intelligent experience and the manifold of intuition that falls short of it are not directly recognised in the schematized categories, yet Kant has admitted that both are essential conditions of that intelligent experience. The former give us our sense-data, and these determine in each case which category is to be applied to them. As to things *per se*, can Kant say that we have literally no knowledge of them? He is certain that they are, and accordingly he applies to them his category of existence (*Dasein*); and in fact, they are always there, so long at least as experience lasts. Further, in maintaining that in sensation they 'affect' us, he also applies to these things *per se* his category of cause. As to sense-data, they cannot be nothing more than utterly undetermined matter, a μὴ ὄν, the bare potentiality of form. To assume this would come very near to saying that after all our intuition is creative and not merely receptive. Further, Kant conceived it possible that our sense-data might not be amenable to any intellectual handling of ours at all[1].

Here then are points of which Kant took no adequate account, clearly involved in his problem though they are. He is continually in his letters and elsewhere emphasizing the appalling complexity of this problem; nevertheless, his final 'summary of the result[2],' the transcendental deduction *in nuce*, reduces the question to a single and seemingly

[1] Cf. *Critique*, A. p. 90=B. p. 123; A. p. 737=B. p. 765. Cf. Dr G. D. Hicks, *op. cit*. pp. 187 ff.

[2] Cf. B. § 27.

simple issue. There are, he says, only two ways conceivable of explaining a *necessary* correspondence between experience and those concepts of its objects which, according to him, we find to be epistemologically *a priori*: either the experience makes these concepts possible, or they make the experience possible. But what objects and what experience? If we go back to sentient experience, then both things *per se* and the sentient subject are involved. As for intelligent experience—we have seen that the sentient experiences which it presupposes cannot be—and according to Kant himself, are not—bare matter, simply the occasion for the exercise of a free hand on the part of intellect. They are potentially already objects to be respected and understood. Here again then we have two essential and cooperant factors. But if we allow that such objects are as yet only potentially objects, *i.e.* not categorial objects, is it not possible that the subject too is still only potentially the self-conscious subject that intelligence implies[1]?

Kant rightly rejects all theories of the exclusively empirical (*i.e. sentient*) origin of concepts as naturalistic—'a sort of *generatio aequivoca*' of pure reason. The other theory—his own alternative—as to their origin, he com-

[1] Kant himself, in fact, as good as admitted that it is no more. Thus (in B. § 15, p. 133) he says: "This reference [to the identity of the subject] does not arise in that I *accompany* every presentation with consciousness" (a phrase denounced by Hegel as barbarous). *Self*-consciousness, that seems to imply, is present as yet only δυνάμει not ἐνεργείᾳ. Cf. A. p. 117 *n. fin.* But this recognition of the gradual development of self-consciousness is most unmistakeably evident in the subjective deduction of his first edition which Kant—unfortunately perhaps—afterwards dropped. Here he tells of a threefold transcendental synthesis, that of 'productive imagination being the most fundamental, and to this, he remarks, "there must come that of apperception [which he goes on to speak of as 'the later and highest'] in order to render the function of the former intellectual" (A. p. 124).

pares to *epigenesis*[1]. This simile, however, so apt in itself, instead of supporting Kant's present contention, militates seriously against it. For the theory of epigenesis, as expounded by his contemporary, Casper Wolff, maintained that the complex organism of the adult is the result of a progressive differentiation of a comparatively simple embryo in an appropriate environment. The dependence on the environment is such that in place of an orthogenetic development abortions or arrested developments result, whenever the environment is abnormal. This theory of epigenesis —now a biological commonplace—was first propounded in opposition to the then dominant theory of preformation which Leibniz had warmly espoused; which Kant, however, professed to repudiate.

Yet his repeated assertions—that the forms of intuition and of thought 'lie ready in the mind,' and are discovered on reflexion to have been potentially *before* experience what they now are actually *in* experience—these suggest preformation, if they suggest anything: they are certainly incompatible with epigenesis. Kant is careful to insist, as Leibniz had done, that there is actually neither intuition nor thought till experience begins; but for experience to begin, it suffices that things *per se* should have given rise to the indispensable matter. The formative process as such depends solely on the factors that 'lie ready in the mind.' Hence it is that when experience is sufficiently advanced, it becomes possible—but then only with pains and after '*long practice*'—to decompose it into the addition (*Zusatz*) which we from ourselves contribute to the primitive matter (*Grundstoff*) which we have 'received[2].' Here Kant con-

---

[1] B. § 27, p. 167. Cf. also *Prolegomena*, § 57, p. 158.
[2] B. pp. 1 f. In that case it was surely imperative for Kant to give a

fuses the issue by introducing the new and very inept analogy of chemical composition, anticipating in a way the mental chemistry of J. S. Mill and others. But it is surely stretching this notion unduly to put process and stuff on a par. Anyhow, it is impossible to equate this chemical, with Kant's other, biological, analogy; yet his use of it is evidence of the preformationism implied both in the subjective as well as in the objective deduction, though explicitly rejected in the latter[1].

If, however,—we may ask again—it was not till experience was very far advanced, and then only by prolonged reflexion, that the *a priori* factors could be abstracted from it, is there any ground for assuming their presence, as what they now are, even from the first? And again is there any warrant for assuming that the objective factor is now, or ever was, in itself entirely devoid of any form or any continuity[2]? But if 'the epigenesis of pure reason' is verily the outcome of Kant's transcendental deduction, then both these assumptions concerning *knowledge* must be denied. The problem is not an antithetic one—a case of 'either… or': the solution is not to be found either in 'reason' alone or in 'matters of fact' alone. The problem is a synthetic one—a case of 'both…and': the solution is to be found neither in reason alone nor in sense-data alone. Know-

precise and adequate account of this analysis so difficult to perform—an analysis—a living and active vivisection even to the dividing both of the joints and marrow of experience—which we remember he has more than once declared we can never completely effect. Cf. p. 25 above.

[1] Cf. B. § 27, pp. 167 ff. But in the *Prolegomena*, § 57, p. 168, he seems to accept preformation and to reject epigenesis.

[2] Kant defines matter—*i.e.* the reflective concept, matter—as the determinable (*Das Bestimmbare*) and form as its determination (*dessen Bestimmung*) and maintains that the very possibility of such 'matter' presupposes formal intuition, so controverting Leibniz (A. pp. 266 ff. = B. pp. 322 ff.).

ledge is not the result of either one of these factors alone: it is the resultant of both.

And this—as we may presently see—is the outcome to which after all Kant's *Critique* as a whole clearly points—provided, that is, we discard certain extreme positions which he was not able consistently to maintain. These are (1) the 'absolute disparateness' of phenomena and things *per se*, (2) the absolute separation of sensibility and understanding, the one purely passive, the other partly spontaneous[1], (3) the absolute distinction of matter and form, and last—but as I believe not least, (4) the assumption that a presentation is 'a subjective modification.'

On the last of these a remark seems called for. Though he constantly spoke of sensations as subjective modifications Kant all the while knew better. He has himself expressly said: "By the word 'sensation' we mean an objective presentation of the senses, and in order not to run the risk of being misunderstood, we shall call by the usual term 'feeling' that which must always remain merely subjective and absolutely cannot constitute a presentation of an object." He then, by way of illustration, contrasts the green colour of a meadow as *objective* with its pleasantness as *subjective*: here the meadow is regarded "as affording satisfaction (*Wohlgefallen*) but this is not a knowledge of it[2]." It was simply preoccupation with the epistemologically objective, presentations that are common property, which misled him—as it has misled so many—into regarding as subjective, objective presentations that are private property, the *peculium* of each individual and so

---

[1] Here indeed he went so far as to allow that "they perhaps may spring from a common but to us unknown root."

[2] *Kritik der Urtheilskraft* (*Werke*, v. § 3, p. 210).

varying from individual to individual[1]. On the *impasse* which thus results I have dwelt at length elsewhere[2].

We must here digress for a moment; for any reference to psychology is sure to call forth an objection which many Kantian commentators are never tired of urging. What Kant meant by *a priori*, we shall be reminded, is not anything psychological at all. "The critical philosophy of Kant," it is said, "recognises no psychology[3]." This can only mean that as regards the main question, *quid juris*, there is—or rather, should be—no appeal to psychology; and that for the simple reason that the preliminary question, *quid facti* is or should be already settled. It ought not to be forgotten that Kant himself repeatedly insisted on this double inquiry and stated plainly that till the first is closed the second cannot be dealt with satisfactorily[4]. His way of handling the prior question, as to the sources (*Quellen*) of the *a priori* was tentative and empirical, as we have already seen: he just reflected, as Locke had done, on what went on in his own mind[5]. But neither he nor Locke realised how much what they called their 'own mind' was what it was in consequence of heredity, tradi-

[1] Cf. *Prolegomena*, § 22, *init.*
[2] Cf. *Naturalism and Agnosticism*, 4th ed. 1915, pp. 408–22. Cf. also Riehl, *Philosophische Kriticismus*, 1887, ii. ii. pp. 53 ff.
[3] Riehl, *Kriticismus*, 1876, i. p. 8. Riehl's own development of this philosophy is itself a refutation of this sweeping statement; but in his second edition he restricts it to the 'main question.'
[4] Cf. *Critique*, A. p. 11 = B. p. 25, referring to the 'sources and limits' of reason; A. p. 84 = B. p. 116, referring to the questions, *quid juris* and *quid facti* and implying that 'proof is demanded of both,' (but cf. especially Preface to the first edition, p. xi); A. p. 154 f. = B. p. 193 f., referring to 'the conditions and extent' of synthetic judgments *a priori*.
[5] "I mean to treat only of reason and its pure thinking, a thorough knowledge of which is not far to seek *since I find it in myself*" (A. Pref. p. viii. Italics mine).

tion and their social environment. The psychology which
in the end he excluded was the psychology which treats
solely of individual experience. But in the case of human
experience it is possible to have a psychology from the
over-individual standpoint of *Bewusstsein überhaupt*, to use
his own term, a 'transcendental psychology' as it has been
proposed to call it. For human experience is not merely
individual, or epistemologically subjective; it is also *trans-
subjective* (or epistemologically objective) which is what
'transcendental' here seems to mean. The failure of Kant's
subjective deduction, with which he was rightly dissatis-
fied, may be traced to such lack of a psychology of 'universal mind.' In his objective deduction he had therefore
to content himself with shewing barely as a matter of fact
the connexion that exists between *a priori*—that is universal and necessary—knowledge and self-consciousness.
All experients, however, are not self-conscious; so, till self-
consciousness is accounted for, that deduction is incom-
plete. It was a true instinct, therefore, that led Kant to
seek first to solve this question of origin. But for the
reasons given he failed, and instead of setting about providing himself with a genuine 'transcendental psychology'
he got lost in a maze of transcendental faculties supposed
to be hidden in the depth of the individual soul; but, in
fact, assumed chiefly because he saw no way of getting
on without them[1].

§ 9. *Kant as the Copernicus of epistemology*

All three of Kant's so-called deductions, the metaphysical, the subjective and the objective, then, turn out

[1] Cf. the writer's *Realm of Ends*, 3rd ed. 1920, pp. 122–8.

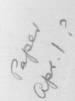

to be faulty. The first in fact is in detail worthless; the second lacks the needful psychological basis and Kant himself was fully conscious of its defects. In the third, the most important and the most ambitious, he would have accomplished more if he had attempted less. In claiming that reason must be *aut Caesar aut nullus*[1] he spoiled a good case for a constitutional monarchy. It is surely passing strange that such incoherent foundations should have seemed to Kant stable enough to sustain this main thesis of his *Critique*, to wit, that "the understanding is itself the law-giver to nature"—a revolution in philosophy which he compared to the Copernican revolution in astronomy[2]. But the comparison is halt and lame save in the one trivial point that the formal conversion of a certain relation between two terms is common to both: the substitution, that is to say, of a $b\mathrm{R}a$ for an $a\mathrm{R}b$. The a and b for Copernicus were two alternative *descriptions* of celestial movements, commonly but not quite accurately called, the geocentric and the heliocentric respectively; for Kant the a and b were two assumable *grounds* of our objective experience, things *per se* and our inherent 'forms' of intuition and thought. The simpler description which Copernicus advocated exalted the universe and humbled the earth: the bold paradox which—'exaggerated and absurd though it sounded[3],' Kant nevertheless attempted to uphold—exalted

[1] Cf. *Prolegomena*, § 10, p. 20.
[2] Cf. A. p. 126 *fin.*; B. Pref. pp. xvi–xxii.
[3] Cf. A. pp. 125–7. The parallel between the intelligible world of the *Dissertation* and the intelligible world restricted to phenomena, which is all that the *Critique* retains, is striking enough to deserve a passing notice. The 'matter' of the noumenal world was substantial entities—monads in fact: the matter of the phenomenal world is a manifold of sensations. These imply space and time, sensible forms which had no application to the noumenal world. But, otherwise, as regards form, the two worlds are alike

the knowing subject and banished beyond the limits of knowledge the whole universe of things *per se*. Copernicus, as Kant remarks, was justified long afterwards by Newton; and he hints that his own ultimate justification will be found; not, however, in the region of theory but in that of practice. Meanwhile he claims that his 'hypothesis' alone accounts for universal and necessary, that is to say, what he called *a priori* knowledge. This claim is all that we have to consider just now. Here not even an epistemological Kepler—to say nothing of an epistemological Newton—has yet appeared. Moreover, as Copernicus did not succeed in entirely dispensing with Ptolemaic epicycles and eccentrics, still less did Kant succeed in freeing his standpoint from the implications of the old naive realism. The *Ding an sich*, in spite of all, is still the Achilles heel of the Critical philosophy.

How then, we naturally inquire, was Kant led to propound thus confidently a thesis apparently so 'extravagant and absurd'? This inquiry leads us back to the working of his mind in 1770, when writing his *Dissertation*. Now, as then, mathematics is the *point d'appui* of his argument. As the forms of intuition yield an *a priori* science of the phenomenal, mathematics; so by parity of reasoning, he then concluded the forms of thought, methodically employed, should yield an *a priori* science of the noumenal, metaphysics. But in the meantime he had come to distinguish between formal and transcendental logic;

inasmuch as the same dynamical categories are present in each. The supreme principle of its form, for the noumenal world is the one God; for the phenomenal world it is the transcendental unity of self-consciousness. The one is creative, the other is only architectonic. God by intellective intuition makes nature as it is; but man whose intuition is only sensitive, still—like a demiurge—shapes nature as it appears to him.

and thus he saw at length that for us the *usus realis* of the understanding implies a content given through sense. He therefore—for the second time and finally—renounced all pretension to a knowledge of the noumenal; for of that we have no intuition. This renunciation breaks down the old barrier between sensibility and understanding: both alike are now confined to knowledge of the phenomenal. The parity of reasoning which dictated the procedure of the *Dissertation* thus becomes more cogent than ever. As the forms of intuition make an *a priori* science, mathematics, possible, may we not 'anticipate' that the pure concepts of the understanding—assumed to be completely ascertained—will in conjunction with mathematics encompass an *a priori* knowledge underlying all possible experience? So it was, then, that Kant proceeded so confidently to formulate the fundamental principles of a pure science of nature not derived from experience but imposed on it.

§ 10. *The fundamental principles of the pure Understanding*

To follow him further it becomes needful at length to take some account of his table of categories. They were divided into two main classes called respectively mathematical and dynamical: the former determining what were called the constitutive, the latter what were called the regulative, principles of possible experience. The constitutive principles, it should be observed, are not themselves mathematical; but assuming the formal validity of pure mathematics as already established, they justify its application to experience, its 'objective' validity. This, Kant maintained, is not a matter of intuition, but pertains

entirely to the understanding. These principles are called
constitutive because they relate to the *content* of experience
as received in the forms of intuition (space and time); and
because concerning the *matter* of experience, sensation,
we can at least anticipate that it will have an intensive
magnitude or degree. These are therefore entitled (1)
Axioms of Intuition, (2) Anticipations of Perception. They
account for the content of experience as so far homo-
geneous and continuous, *i.e.* as having extensive magnitude
(spatially and temporally) and intensive magnitude, the
degree in which sensibility is affected.

The regulative principles, on the other hand, are not
concerned with this sensory continuum as such. They
also fall under two heads entitled (1) Analogies of Experience, (2) The Postulates of Empirical Thinking in
general. But the latter we may safely ignore: they are
simply dragged in to fill up a gap Kant had left by introducing *modality* into his table of judgments. In fact they
are merely definitions of possibility, actuality, and necessity[1]; and, so far, have no title to be called categories at
all; for they are not forms of synthetic unity[2]. The
Analogies of Experience on the other hand, deal with the
real categories which are supposed to make any intelligible
experience possible. For these—and only for these—Kant
propounds a general principle, *viz.* that "all phenomena,
as regards their existence (*Dasein*) are subject *a priori* to
rules determining their relation, one to another, in one

[1] In this respect, as we shall see, they are important enough.
[2] If the 'postulates' they are supposed to yield were principles, Kant
would have felt bound to offer not an elucidation of them—which is all
he gives—but a demonstration, as in the case of the rest. Here, as in so
many places, Kant, like the hero of Mrs. Shelley's *Frankenstein*, is just the
slave of his own invention.

time[1]." Not the *a priori* content of phenomena as *existing*
then, we now see, but their *a priori* relations to each other,
is the topic of these dynamical principles, which 'first of
all make a Nature possible[2].' The special principles treat
severally of the relation of Substance and Accident, of the
relation of Cause and Effect, and of the Reciprocal Interaction (*commercium dynamicum*) of substances *inter se*.
These principles are not called axioms, because they do
not, like the constitutive principles, relate to what is
intuitively evident: they are only discursive, directing us
to seek a rule determining the connexion of one empirical
fact with another. Kant, accordingly, occasionally speaks
of them as anticipations[3].

But the difference between his constitutive and his
regulative principles is for epistemology a radical one and
Kant in the *Critique* made far too light of it. It recalls the
distinction Locke and Hume had already drawn between
relations of ideas and relations of matters of fact. The
former yield strictly universal and necessary propositions.
The latter, though equally certain in the particular
instances observed—and though they give rise to a subjective 'anticipation,' which is strengthened by every recurrence till it too becomes at length practically certain—
still never yield a necessary proposition; they can, therefore, never yield a strictly universal one. All this, we
remember, Kant had fairly recognised in his pre-critical
period[4], and his frequent use of 'anticipation' in this con-

[1] A. p. 176 *fin.*=B. p. 218.   [2] B. p. 263.
[3] Cf. above, p. 63; also B. pp. 264, 303. Hence it was that Kant
bethought him of calling them *analogies,* since their procedure resembles—
albeit only superficially—the mathematical procedure in ascertaining a
proportion: there a number is found, here a relation is only sought.
[4] Cf. pp. 18 f. above.

nexion might have led him to pause; yet, on the strength of his transcendental deduction, he ignores it all now. "The synthetic principles of the understanding, he now maintains, are the necessary conditions of *the possibility of experience at all*, and therefore of *the possibility of the objects of experience* themselves as such[1]." Had he been content with saying that they are a *sine qua non* of *systematic* experience nobody perhaps would object. But he went much further than this. "The understanding," he roundly maintained, "is itself the source of the laws of nature.... All empirical laws are only special determinations of the pure laws of the understanding[2]."

The section entitled "Of the Supreme Principle of all synthetical judgments," referred to above, fundamental though it is for Kant's whole theory of knowledge, is one of the most vulnerable in his so-called *Analytic of Principles*. In the first place, we note that he here simply flies in the face of facts by ignoring the genetic continuity of experience widely understood, and forgets, *more suo*, much that he had already admitted elsewhere. Apart from the systematized experience obtained through the real categories he now can find nothing left save what he fancifully styles 'a rhapsody of perceptions, which is not knowledge (*Erkenntniss*) and could never yield an altogether coherent consciousness.' How in that case the behaviour of the lower animals, the gradual advance of every normal child and of the human race as a whole from such a beginning to 'the age of reason,' he never even dreamt of explaining.

[1] Cf. A. pp. 154–8 = B. pp. 193–7, here summarised.
[2] A. p. 127 *fin*. Cf. also *Prolegomena*, § 35, "The understanding has with entire freedom taken its fundamental principles from itself"; and § 36, "*The understanding derives its laws* (a priori) *not from nature but prescribes them to it*." Italics Kant's own.

WK

In short for Kant, as we have indeed already seen, there *was* no continuity known to exist between sensibility and understanding, between judgments of perception and judgments of experience.

In the next place, the phrase 'possibility of experience' —which is the key to Kant's whole position and specially prominent here—also calls for some comment. In the *Prolegomena* (§ 36), however, Kant formulates the substance of this section more concisely, and also more definitely: so we may refer to that. "How is nature itself possible?" This is the question he is discussing. On its *material* side, 'by means of the constitution (*Beschaffenheit*) of *our* sensibility as affected by *objects*'—is the answer. Here then we have an explicit recognition of the duality of experience in its first and wider sense, and Kant should hold fast to that. But if experience implies both subject and object, its possibility must involve the *existence* of both. The existence of the subject, however, will not account for that of the object; nor, *vice versa*, the existence of the object for that of the subject. Further, if by 'laws' we understand whatever the existence of the object involves, laws in this sense cannot be due to the subject. Similarly the existence of the subject involves certain functions, which—as such—cannot be due to the object, *e.g.* sensibility, activity, plasticity. Nevertheless the actual exercise (ἐνέργεια) of these functions (δύναμεις) of the subject is first called forth by the actuality of the object in affecting it. Such is briefly the duality of experience which Kant begins by allowing.

On the *formal* side the answer is not so simple. There is, Kant maintains, '*a necessary agreement* (*Uebereinstimmung*) *between the principles of possible experience and the laws of the possibility of nature*[1].' The question now is, How is this agreement to be explained? Here we need first to be clear about the meaning of 'possibility'—the term which divided Kant first of all from the Leibniz-Wolffian school. He used it, as they did, in the logical sense of freedom from contradiction. But he rejected their view that the possible can be determined independently of the actual. Here, then, where not logical but real possibility is in question, the actual must be implied. In his first postulate[2] Kant gives the following definition of real possibility: "What agrees with the formal conditions of experience (in respect of intuition and concepts) is possible." There is no overt reference to actuality in this: it seems to be merely an analytical statement of what possibility of experience means. Applying this definition to nature, that too may be called 'possible' provided it agrees with the formal conditions of experience. And obviously two things—experience and nature—which agree with the same thing must agree with each other.

So we come now to the question: how is this agreement to be explained? For Kant, as we have seen, these were but the two alternatives: either we learn from nature in the course of experience what its universal laws are, or we ourselves impose these laws upon it in accordance with principles (or conditions) which make experience possible. The former alternative he rejects as *self-contradictory*; but only by covertly begging the question at issue, for an open contradiction could hardly be entertained as a genuine alternative. The conditions or principles of experience, he says, are not due to nature, "because the universal laws of

---

[1] *Prolegomena*, p. 112. Italics mine.
[2] A. p. 218 = B. p. 265.

nature can and must be known *a priori*." But we recall
that for Kant behind all this possibility actuality is involved; and that, regarding nature on its material side, he
himself admitted the duality in unity of experience, the
interaction, that is to say, of objects affecting and subject
responding.

For Kant, however, nature and the objects affecting the
subject are by no means the same. 'Objective reality,' in
fact, is one of Kant's treacherous phrases. It sometimes
refers to things *per se* as in his account of the material side
of nature; but when as here the formal side is in question,
the reference is not to things *per se* but to their effects—
to phenomena as subjective. So, for example, in this very
section[1]: "If a knowledge is to have any objective reality
...the object must necessarily be given in some way or
other." But in 'explaining' the first postulate Kant
broaches a third meaning of objective reality. So far as the
a priori is concerned, objective reality means the same as
transcendental truth[2]; and transcendental truth, he elsewhere observes, 'precedes all empirical truth [or know-
ledge] and renders it possible[3].' Here the real has again
dropped out of sight never again to return. "Nature and
possible experience," Kant winds up by saying, "are
entirely one and the same[4]." The two necessarily corresponding possibilities merge into one. And after all, this
is what the attempt absolutely to separate what we call
appearances from that which appears must come to at
last. Yet these things *per se* were indispensable all the
while: they alone provide the stuff out of which the experience we call nature is supposed to be independently

[1] A. p. 155 = B. p. 194.   [2] A. p. 222 = B. p. 269.
[3] A. p. 146 = B. p. 185.   [4] *Prolegomena, loc. cit.* p. 113

framed. Do they do no more than provide the stuff? This is what we have to see.

In a passage *à propos* specially of causation, Kant takes the dilemma by the horns, which he perhaps saw might be awaiting him. Referring to the general position enounced above he begins by saying: "This seems indeed to contradict all that has ever been observed concerning the progress of our understanding, *viz.* that it was only through induction that laws were first of all discovered and the concept of *cause* came to be framed." This was Hume's position of course. "In which case," he then continues, "that concept would be only empirical and the rules which it provides devoid of all universality and necessity. In point of fact, however, as with other *a priori* presentations (*e.g.* space and time) so here: we can only separate them out of experience as clear concepts, because we had [previously] put them in. It is doubtless true that the logical clearness of this presentation as a concept of cause only becomes possible after we have made use of it in experience (as a rule determining a series of events); but some regard to it (*eine Rücksicht auf dieselbe*) as [a] condition of the synthetic unity of phenomena in time was still the ground of the experience itself and therefore preceded it *a priori*[1]."

This not very lucid passage seems important as furnishing—better than many—a central text for comment on Kant's Copernican position, *viz.* that the pure science of nature is the creation of the understanding, not derived from nature but prescribed to it. As to the first part of it, controverting Hume, it must be at once admitted that there are no laws of nature that are real and at the same

[1] A. pp. 195 f. = B. pp. 240 f., somewhat condensed.

time necessary and universal, none to which the possibility of exception would imply a contradiction. Has Kant, has anybody ever been able to adduce a single real law of which this cannot be said? All such laws of nature are only generalisations, have only what Kant himself called 'comparative universality.' As to a necessary and universal science of nature cognate with mathematics, Kant has failed entirely to shew that any such science exists[1]. 'General physics'—or as we now say, Dynamics—he allows is largely mathematical, is in fact scientific just in so far as it *is* mathematical[2]. But then it is not an entirely pure science; for it involves concepts such as motion, impenetrability and inertia. Moreover, it is not a universal science, for it takes account only of the objects of external sense. A science of nature in general to deserve the name must bring the objects both of physics and of psychology under universal laws[3]. This 'strictly pure and universal science of nature as a system,' or 'metaphysic of nature is,' however, he tells us, "entirely separate from mathematics, and is not comparable with this as a means of enlarging our insight [into facts]; but nevertheless it is very important in the criticism of the pure knowledge of the understanding which is to be applied to nature in general[4]." The pure science (or metaphysic) of nature is then not on a par with mathematics but ranks epistemologically above it, controlling and criticizing its application to nature[5].

---

[1] We find him, however, assuming it. Cf. B. p. 127 *fin*.
[2] *Metaphysische Anfangsgründe der Naturwissenschaft* (*Werke*, IV. p. 360).
[3] *Prolegomena*, §§ 15, 23.
[4] A. p. 847 *n.* = B. p. 875 *n*.
[5] The complications and confusions of Kant's 'architectonic of the pure

How then could Kant assert or assume that we are actually in possession of a pure or *a priori* science of nature grounded *like mathematics* on universal and necessary concepts and principles? The concepts of mathematics he held to be exact and definable and its principles all either axiomatic or demonstrable. In contrast with this, however, he has said that "speaking accurately...substance and cause cannot be defined"; and again, "that whereas mathematics, because working with intuitions, can have axioms, philosophy, because working with concepts, has no principle worthy the name of axiom[1]."

This brings us to the second part of our text. According to that, though we are said to derive the category of cause from experience, yet we do so only because we had previously introduced it into experience, thereby in fact first rendering experience possible. Nevertheless the logical clearness of this concept, which we eventually recover only by reflexion, presupposes the use said to be made of it in empirical rules 'determining series of events.' We naturally look then for some account of what has

reason' are discussed at length by Vaihinger (*Commentar*, 1. pp. 304–10). They are, however, too appalling for treatment here.

[1] Cf. *Critique*, A. pp. 728, 732 = B. pp. 756, 760. In one curious passage—after displaying his table of categories in orderly array—he remarks: "I intentionally omit here the definitions of these categories, though I may be in possession of them....At present they would only divert us from the main point of our investigation" (A. p. 82 *fin.* = B. p. 108 *fin.*). In a later passage—after completing that investigation—he remarks: "Above, in the exposition of the categories, we dispensed with the definition of each of them, because it seemed unnecessary for our purpose, which concerned only their synthetical use....Now, however, it is apparent that this caution had even a deeper ground, to wit that *we could not have defined them even if we had wished*; since they could have neither meaning nor applicability apart from sensibility," *i.e.* from their use in experience, in other words, as schematized. (A. p. 241; italics mine. This passage is omitted in B!)

supervened between the introduction of that, which was at first but a confused concept, and its abstraction later on, as the 'logically clear' concept of the relation of Cause and Effect. If rules, which only now suggest this concept to us, were an indispensable preliminary to its logical distinctness, how can Kant be so confident that what we take out is no more than what we first put in? If a baker were to maintain that he only draws a batch of loaves from his oven because he first put them in, even that would not be as equivocal a statement as this one of Kant's; for the baker at least put in the dough himself. Should we not rather assume that as the fire for the baking of the bread; so the miscalled 'things *per se*' for experience were an essential factor in its development? But let us look closer.

Kant admits that the rules are found before the causal category is consciously applied. In that case we have what he called a 'perception judgment,' as *e.g.* whenever the sun shines we observe that the stones become warm[1]. So far the recurrence of a certain time-order is simply perceived; but the pure understanding has so far contributed nothing. And the time order was a *given* order. For, even were we to grant—as Kant assumed—that our apprehension is always successive, still, as he points out, it is sometimes arbitrary, as, *e.g.*, in perceiving one after another the parts of a house. In that case the order of apprehension is subjectively determined; but in other cases, as, *e.g.*, in our apprehension of the successive positions of a ship drifting downstream, the order is not arbitrary: it is objectively determined. And such are the cases in which repetition evokes a rule: we do not however produce the rule, we only reproduce it in memory after it has been

[1] Cf. *Prolegomena*, §§ 18, 19 *n*.

given. So then without any intervention of the category of causality, transforming temporal sequence, *id post hoc*, into real consequence, *id propter hoc*, we find already, in our individual experience, rules—forewarning and forearming —which guide our actions in daily life. And further than this at the perceptual level we never go. "Here then," as Kant himself naively remarks—naively, I say, in view of his Copernican standpoint—"there is, to be sure, as yet no necessary synthesis, and therefore no concept of cause[1]." This remark he makes *à propos* of the so-called perceptual judgment just now quoted. But, he continues—if instead of merely perceiving that "whenever the sun shines the stones become warm"—we had asserted that "the sun is ...the cause of the warmth," we should have an 'experience judgment,' by which he meant a judgment made at the conceptual level[2], the level of universal experience or *Bewusstsein überhaupt*. Thereby, at any rate, the empirical rule—the rule of experience at the perceptual level, the level, that is to say of merely individual experience, would, he tells us, be 'raised to the dignity' of a causal law.

But this is surely going too fast: we want to know more about these two kinds of judgment. At the lower level rules are simply found: we act in accord with them but we do not reflect about them. At the higher level rules are sought, because if experience is to become systematic, rules that are known to be rules, that is laws, must be found. Now the understanding, Kant tells us, is specially the faculty of rules in this sense: "It is always busy in thoroughly prying into phenomena for the very purpose of discovering some rule or other among them[3]."

---

[1] *Prolegomena*, § 29, p. 100.   [2] *Prolegomena*, § 20 *n*.
[3] A. p. 126. He has also said, and seemingly forgotten, that "the under-

Again we may ask is such a procedure suggestive of legislating? Anyhow such search surely implies that at this level—having reflected—we have got at length some idea of the sort of rule we seek: otherwise search would surely be impossible. How did we come by this idea? The particular phenomena to which the causal category is to be applied are cases of change; but of change, Kant admitted, nothing could be known *a priori*. How then can his second analogy which is exclusively concerned with changes be independent of experience? In expounding the 'anticipations of perception' Kant asserts definitely that the causality of change as such is a problem beyond the limits of transcendental philosophy, because it presupposes empirical principles[1]. But for this it would, he says, be easy to demonstrate mathematically that all change is continuous. When he comes to the exposition of this second analogy, however, where causality is regarded as the principle of the filling of time,—and so must be conceived as continuous—he is driven to connect the continuity of change with the continuity of our apprehension of succession[2]!

§ 11. *The Copernican Standpoint not sustained*

It seems surely clearer than ever that the sense-*knowledge* which renders experience at the perceptual level possible is also a *sine qua non* of that higher phase of experience in which thought-knowledge is essential. And this priority

standing is capable of being instructed and equipped by means of rules." A. p. 133 = B. p. 172.

[1] Cf. also B. p. 3, and with this p. 5.

[2] A. pp. 171 f., B. p. 213 *init*. Cf. Professor Norman Smith's *Commentary*, pp. 380 ff.

of the perceptual to the conceptual, Kant, when all is said
and done, does actually, as indeed he must, concede. Not
merely so. He even goes out of his way to imagine—as he
thinks we quite well can—a situation in which phenomena
might be such as to suffice for perceptual experience and
yet leave the conceptual relation of cause and effect
"empty, null and meaningless[1]"—a situation indeed to
which all but a small minority of the human race are
practically confined, the vast multitude who never get
beyond empirical rules having only comparative gener-
ality, never attain the concept of universal and necessary
laws regarded as valid *a priori*. How come there to be
such empirical rules? Phenomena embody them, but do
not explain them, any more than they explain themselves.
But if the existence of phenomena is inexplicable apart
from what Kant called things *per se*—and that he never
for a moment doubted—can those empirical rules, which
at the perceptual level we do not seek but merely find, be
explicable apart from those same things *per se*? If we must
fall back on them to account for the *Dasein*, the existence
of what we have got into the way of calling phenomena,
can their *Sosein*, their relations to each other, be accounted
for otherwise[2]? On the contrary, is it not perfectly obvious

[1] Cf. A. p. 90 = B. p. 123; *Krit. d. Urtheilskraft*, p. 191 *fin.*
[2] Some of Kant's commentators have endeavoured to save him by point-
ing out that he only maintained the *Dasein* of things *per se* (as accounting
for the existence of phenomena) and that after all existence is not a predicate.
Cf. B. Erdmann, *Kant's Kriticismus in der ersten und in der zweiten
Auflage*, 1878, pp. 40 ff., 47. But Höffding, who discusses the relation
of phenomena and things *per se* at some length (*Geschichte der neueren
Philosophie*, 1896, II. pp. 62–6), cites one passage in which Kant has said:
"To the transcendental object we can ascribe the whole *extent and connexion* (*Umfang und Zusammenhang*) of our possible percepts, and say
that before all experience it is given *per se*; and *conformably to it all phenomena* are *given* in experience" (A. p. 494 = B. p. 522; italics mine). Here

that the continuity which holds in the one case must hold also in the other? Is not our knowledge of what we call nature in both alike just so much knowledge of these so-called things *per se*? And now, if we do not set out to seek for laws till this Nature has educated us sufficiently by empirical rules, can we with any sense or modesty pretend to be her lawgiver, prescribing *a priori* what are to be inviolable laws for her? No wonder then that Jacobi after long study of the *Critique* confessed, that *without* the thing *per se* he could find no way into the system, and *with* it, found it impossible to remain there. With this dilemma Kant himself strove hard to deal: and many an anxious hour it must have cost him, as the vacillations in his second edition and the controversies of his commentators plainly shew. That he failed to sustain his Copernican standpoint few would question; but that he accomplished nothing important by his transcendental philosophy perhaps no one would affirm. However before attempting to estimate his positive contributions under this head it will be well briefly to summarize the results of our discussion of it thus far.

On two points Kant has been censured for his prejudices or prepossessions (*Vorurtheile*)—we might even say they were obsessions—the first in respect of mathematics; the second in respect of his so-called 'pure' science of nature. These two are closely connected. But I think we must add a third,—in respect of formal logic.

Beginning with the first—we recall how strenuously in his pre-critical phase Kant had insisted on the radical

we have *Sosein* as well as *Dasein* attributed not indeed directly to things *per se*, but to the transcendental object which, at first at any rate, for Kant implied them. And other passages of a like intent might be quoted.

distinctions that mark off mathematics as at once exact and formal from all branches of philosophy dealing with reality. Yet in the *Dissertation* and even in the *Critique* he so far ignored this difference as to treat mathematics as, so to say, the paradigm of the *a priori* and attempt to bring the philosophy of nature into line. Yet a similar difference, he allowed, still divided his constitutive principles as axiomatic from the regulative principles which were only discursive. But mathematical concepts are not merely intuitive constructions, they are also, in consequence of this, concrete individuals in a sense in which real, *i.e.* empirical, concepts never are. It may seem paradoxical to say that they are individual because they are universal, whereas the concepts of natural science are never individual because they are always only general, concerned with existing things, and that in a way in which the concepts of mathematics are not. Yet this is a truth which Kant has never disallowed. Moreover all his synthetic principles are stated as general propositions[1]. As such they may be only discursive but cannot in any case be pure or *a priori* in the sense in which mathematical propositions are. Even these, when *applied* to empirical facts are *pro tanto* divested of their pure, ideal or archetypal character[2]. There are, in short, no *a priori* facts.

Nevertheless Kant placed mathematics and what he called pure natural science on a par, 'brought metaphysics into the good company of mathematics' as he once said[3]. This was the other of his unwarrantable 'prepossessions.' According to this, either the mathematics must be applied

---

[1] The so-called 'postulates' are an exception, but they—we have seen reason to think—are not synthetic principles.

[2] Kant's frequent confusion of pure and applied mathematics is notorious.

[3] *Prolegomena*, § 4.

or the natural science must be formal. But whereas mathematics for Kant was constructive, because its domain was that of pure intuition, philosophy could never be constructive, because it dealt solely with the real—of which we at least have no such intuition. Even the constructions of mathematics he declared would be but 'figments of the brain' if they could not be applied. But at any rate these figments are all the exact knowledge we have, and philosophy—as Kant alternately proclaimed and forgot—has none such. There is then no pure science of nature as real. How then came Kant to be obsessed with a belief in such a science? He misunderstood Newton as Newton was commonly misunderstood down almost to our own time. He argued as if Newton's *Principia* were concerned with substances and causes, whereas Newton's aim was rather, in the now classic language of Kirchhoff, merely "to describe in the exactest and completest manner such motions as occur in nature." Epistemologically regarded, there is then strictly speaking nothing in common between Immanuel Kant's 'pure science of nature' and the *Principia* of Isaac Newton. For Newton mathematics waited on physics, *i.e.* on experience. As is well known he refrained for years from enouncing his theory of gravitation because it was at variance with what were erroneously supposed to be facts. But for Kant mathematics, as we remember, he expressly said, waited on *meta*physics by which its application was to be controlled. Accordingly between the two editions of his *Critique* he produced a new and metaphysical *Principia*, into which the whole of Newton's *Principia* was absorbed[1], and an *a priori* basis

---

[1] This work, entitled *The metaphysical Rudiments of Natural Science* (1786)—as we might expect from the fact that here we have Newton's

provided for facts such as inertia, mass, impenetrability, the equality of action and reaction, etc.

The third of Kant's *vorgefasste Meinungen* was his persistent inability to realise effectively the limitations of the old formal logic, although in his pre-critical period he was already aware of it[1]. Though discerning, as he did, the cardinal importance of his own transcendental logic, which is never formal but always functional, he still proclaimed his adherence to the method of Wolff and fills a whole page with lavish praise of this 'prime inspirer of German thoroughness[2].' And, in fact, throughout the *Critique* itself he seems to be always striving to reach the actual through the possible as logically defined, while yet rejecting the rationalistic position that the really possible can be defined independently of the actual.

§ 12. *What remains*

Setting all these indefensible prepossessions aside, we may now inquire what remains of permanent value in the transcendental philosophy. What remains is—as we noted at the outset—that in this philosophy the one-sided extremes of rationalism and empiricism find at length a

Principia set out in 'metaphysical guise'— is full of that surreptitious importation of the empirical which we have already noted as characteristic of Kant's other master, Wolff (cf. above, p. 10). It is not without incidental merits—what work of Kant's is? But it has had practically no influence, where Galileo and Newton have produced a revolution, that is to say, in natural science; and it has deservedly been passed over for the most part by philosophers. And yet, if this neglect—as in the parallel but far more flagrant instance of Hegel's *Naturphilosophie*—has helped to safeguard the philosophers' reputation, it has hindered the formation of a correct estimate of the value of their philosophy as a whole—of which the pure science of nature is one of the weakest parts.

[1] Cf. above, pp. 17 f.   [2] B. Pref. pp. xxxvi f.

meeting-place. Like 'the double images' of a drunken Philip—to recall our figure—these half-images of the full reality are unified in the vision of a Philip that is sober. For rationalism could not reconcile its principle of Identity and Contradiction with that of Sufficient Ground, its truths of reason with its truths of fact—in other words could not focus its *lumen naturale.* As little could empiricism with its *tabula rasa* account for the presence in experience of such concepts as substance and cause, which none the less it could not disown. Kant, probably not without the help of Leibniz's *nisi intellectus ipse*, disposed —as we may see—of the empirical deadlock with its threat of scepticism; and certainly aided by 'the spark Hume had struck' he exposed the fallacy of rationalism which was wrecking philosophy on the arid shoals of mere formalism.

Now, however, by a single principle Kant opened up for philosophy a renewed and fruitful career—by the central truth, I mean, which he called the synthetic unity of apperception. Objective experience structurally regarded, is, as he pointed out, from end to end a synthesis of what he termed 'a manifold[1].' This synthesizing or integrating process is begun at the lower or perceptual level of experience and continued at the higher or intellectual level, solely by the interested, the living, activity of the experient subject itself. But it is with the intellectual synthesis that we are now chiefly concerned. Here we find Kant propounding an entirely new theory of knowledge. Unhappily he was too fascinated by the false yet flashy

---

[1] A manifold, however, which he neglected to notice is never entirely disconnected, but is, like what he called its pure forms—space and time— always a continuum which is gradually differentiated.

glamour of his metaphysical deduction to see quite clearly all that his transcendental synthesis based on the functional unity of self-consciousness in knowing really meant. Had he but kept steadfastly to this, his fundamental standpoint, he could never have imagined that the *meaning* of substance, cause, and interaction was either derived from or contained in the bare logical forms of the categorical, the hypothetical, and the disjunctive propositions respectively. And in fact, as we shall see, he did not really imagine this. Already in the *Dissertation* he had distinguished between the logical and the real employment of intellect, and assigned these categories exclusively to the latter. There they were the categories constitutive of the knowledge of the intelligible world as it is in itself. In the *Critique*— though now only rules for the pursuit of knowledge about this world as it appears to us—they are still the real categories without which no experience above the perceptual level would be possible. Both in the *Dissertation* and in the *Critique* these categories were regarded as jointly and severally involved in the idea of the world as a whole—as it *is* in the first, as it *appears* to us in the second. Causality implies action (*Handlung*) action again implies power (*Kraft*), or as we now say energy as actual, and not merely potential; and so we are led back to Substance to which this energy belongs. Since the world as a whole is just the mutual interaction of substances that are also causes (*Ursachen*) these two categories, Substance and Cause are all we have now specially to consider.

But if formal logic is not the source of these categories whence then are they ultimately derived? From what the experient subject is and at the intellectual level knows itself to be. This seems to be the true answer, and it is the answer which really underlies the whole of Kant's 'trans-cendental deduction' in its final form[1]. In the very first sections, the synthesis that all experience involves is traced to the activity of the experiencing subject, which itself persists as 'one and the same' throughout. This unity is not for Kant—as some would maintain—the result of the synthesis of the manifold which is unified. It is not to be confused with the *category* of unity but is, he held—as we have already seen—itself the ground and presupposition of all categories; and therefore of these supreme cate-gories—substance and cause[2]. Even in the first edition Kant refers this unity of apperception to the 'permanent and unchanging Ego (*das stehende und bleibende Ich*) which constitutes the correlate of all our presentations.' It was as such that he styled it the transcendental subject and came to speak of a transcendental object as its counter-part or correlate. All this, be it remarked, is said before the co-operation of the categories is mentioned at all[3]. Must we not then conclude that Kant's transcendental deduction clearly points to the experient subject as the source whence these real categories of substance and cause are in fact 'deduced'? In maintaining these categories to be indis-pensable to the possibility of any intelligible experience

[1] Yet, at the very time when he was elaborating this, Kant in his lectures was still teaching not merely that "the Ego is the one case where we can intuite substance immediately...but what is more, the concept, which we have of all things generally, is derived from this Ego." (Cf. M. Heinze's *Vorlesungen Kants über Metaphysik*, as reprinted from the *Proceedings of the Saxon R. S.*, 1914, p. 543.)

[2] Cf. B. §§ 15, 16. But an earlier and very emphatic passage is still worth quoting: "*It* [the Ego] *does not know* itself *through the categories* but knows the *categories* only—and through them all objects—in the absolute unity of apperception, and so *through itself*" (A. p. 402; italics Kant's).

[3] Cf. A. p. 123 *fin.*

of the world is Kant not really maintaining that the world is *intelligible* only when it is interpreted in terms of what the experient subject at the transsubjective and self-conscious level knows itself to be? On what other grounds can it be assumed that the transcendental object or Non-ego, so far from being utterly alien, is verily the Ego's own correlate?

There is, however, one important fact of experience that Kant in common with the psychologists of his day completely overlooked—a fact which strengthens the analogy between these correlatives. The fact, I mean, that the activity of the subject is not confined to the synthesis of sense-data, is never merely cognitive but always and from the first conative and reactive as well. In our intercourse with the external world we have limbs which the Ego controls as well as senses which the Non-ego affects. Herein Kant's third real category is exemplified; and this is in fact the most concrete of the three, since all experience involves the duality and interaction of subject and object. Now movement—according to Kant himself—is the only form in which we can intuite the interaction of external bodies *inter se*[1]. But further, it is only by the movements of our own bodies that we can directly interfere with the course of events; and apart from such intervention we should, as Leibniz put it, be 'deserters from the general order.' A very little reflexion might have convinced Kant that the mere intuition of motion could never have called forth the category of causal connexion, were it not for our action or '*Handlung*' in initiating our own bodily movements. Those intuitional components—contiguity in time and space—Hume had fully recognised:

[1] Cf. B. p. 291.

it was just the 'causal nexus' which he failed to find. Here Schopenhauer saw further than Kant. Whereas Kant contemplated the world exclusively in terms of 'presentation,' Schopenhauer insisted on regarding it primarily in terms of what he called 'will,' meaning thereby just this joint category of substantial cause which we are now considering[1]. We perceive the movements of our own bodies as we perceive those of other bodies, but the former are the only movements that we control immediately and initiate, so to say, from within. This immediate knowledge which we all have of operations due to our own *Wesen* or *esse* we, according to Schopenhauer, 'analogically transfer' to the operations of other things which we can intuite only as 'given external phenomena[2].' The fact that we first fully realise what energy (*Kraft*) means when we find our own movements inhibited, when the object or *Gegenstand* that we perceive is also an obstacle or *Widerstand* which resists—this all-important psychological fact Kant seems to have overlooked altogether. And yet it brings subject and object—Ego and non-Ego—into a real relationship incompatible with the Cartesian dualism, that remnant of rationalism to which Kant was too much inclined to cling.

One of the earliest defects in the transcendental philosophy singled out by opponents and adherents alike was just this failure to hold fast to its central fact, the original synthetic unity of apperception—for, let us not forget—it is a fact, not a mere proposition. Kant's first concern, it was urged[3], should have been to ascertain how experience

---

[1] For substantiality he declared was through and through causality and the principle of causality was that *operari sequitur esse*.

[2] Cf. *Fragmente zur Geschichte der Philosophie*, § 13, "Noch einige Erläuterungen zur Kantischen Philosophie," *Werke*, 1874, v. p. 100.

[3] By Reinhold, Beck and Fichte.

has developed from this centre and all that such development from a single source implies. But Kant did not
altogether escape the eclectic tendencies of his time: so,
between his acceptance wholesale of its faculty-psychology
and his Wolffian bias towards formal logic, he lost sight of
his central theme. The gradually unfolding stem of experience was hidden by its own branches; so much so
that Kant seriously doubted if there were a single stem at
all, nay, began by asserting that there was not. Beginning his
Critique by confining his attention to sensation[1], and accepting unquestioned the psychological theory—then in vogue
—of an internal sense co-ordinate with the external senses,
Kant proceeded without misgiving to regard the transcendental object and the transcendental subject as if they
were entirely on a par. In both cases alike, he felt compelled to trace to an unknowable X concealed behind each
of the two kinds of so-called phenomena, the 'affections'
of the internal and external senses. "The transcendental
object," he said roundly, "is equally unknown in the case
of internal as well as in that of external intuition[2]."

Already we have had to ask the question asked so often:
how could an X be absolutely unknowable and yet be
even thought as a cause[3]? And now further we have to
ask: how could the concept of cause emerge, if we start
from a bare 'manifold' of sensations that could not be
even described as consisting of *effects* without implying a
cause or causes—albeit, as simply 'given,' they could of
themselves imply nothing? And yet what more is there, if
subject and object are alike unknowable and problematic?
When, however, we recognise that by sensory *datum* we

---

[1] Cf. A. pp. 21 f. = B. pp. 35 f.   [2] A. p. 372 *fin.*
[3] Cf. above, p. 53.

mean not merely something *there* or 'tabled'—as Locke
might have said—but something acknowledged as *agendum*
to be dealt with, is it not obvious that an experience which
is both active and receptive implies two efficient causes or
agents within it, is, in fact, just such an interaction as—
according to Kant's third analogy—all our experience is?
In correlating transcendental subject and transcendental
object, he made a good start. This again was essentially
just the recognition of the duality of subject and object as
the ground of all finite experience. Kant failed nevertheless
to realise that this relation is *not* a symmetrical one.
Experience implies the real existence both of subject and
object and a certain *mutuum commercium* between them,
as Kant allowed. Still the nature of the transcendental
object, *i.e.* the whole objective situation, is in itself independent of and indifferent towards, all experients alike.
There is, as Kant himself said, one world for all. Subjects
on the other hand are many; and though they are all
interested in this one world, yet it is the nature of each
that determines its own individual interest in, and therefore its characteristic behaviour towards, the one objective
world. The same situation, which gives rise to appetition
in one, leads to aversion in another while it leaves a third
indifferent and unconcerned. It is this positive selection[1]
that differentiates the rôle of the subjective factor which
Kant recognised as involved in all finite experience.

---

[1] What we call natural selection is obviously not the counterpart of this.
Not only is it essentially negative—merely blind elimination of the unfit;
but it too seems to be ultimately determined—*viz.* by faulty adjustment—
from the subjective side.

§ 13. *Kant's system a philosophical anthropomorphism*

If we now follow up the development of experience from this standpoint of subjective selection we may hope to see clearly that Kant's transcendental synthesis really carries us back to the actual subject of experience as the source of the real categories, substance and cause. If so, their origin will prove to be not logomorphic—to coin a word—but anthropomorphic, not a logical form but a subjective 'analogy.' Kant's use of this term to denote the principles on which the possibility of experience depends would then turn out to have a significance far deeper than any that he himself allowed.

The earliest subjective analogy that the student of anthropology observes is that by which we come to recognise our fellow creatures as other selves, as 'ejects' and not merely as objects. And this analogy comparative psychologists for the most part assume to be foreshadowed in the instinctive behaviour of all but the lowest animals, all that seek their mates and provide for their young. But to the primitive human mind not only their fellow-men but any objects in their environment—the movements of which are specially interesting—appear to be animated and active: the wind bloweth where it listeth, the clouds chase each other across the sky, the wild cataract leaps in glory, and even the weariest river winds somewhere safe to sea. Not only the savage and the poet live in an anthropomorphic world: philosophers, early and late, live there too. Plato has his μῦθοι as well as his λόγος. Even in our own day we have Hegel describing the moon as 'a waterless crystal which seeks to still its thirst and so sets up the tides[1].' But let us return to Kant: we shall find that he is by no means an exception.

In the transcendental philosophy there is a certain anthropomorphism which is openly avowed and defended. It will now be my aim to shew that this anthropomorphism is more thoroughgoing than Kant himself supposed; for he does not himself mention it till he reaches the third and last class of what he called 'the elements of pure reason[2].' Then, having dealt in his *Analytic* with the second of these, the categories of the understanding which he fancied he could trace to the forms of judgment, he comes in the *Dialectic* to the last, the Ideas of the reason, which he still more fancifully traced to the forms of syllogism. If the metaphysical deduction of the categories was worthless *a fortiori* is this of the Ideas[3]. But for these as for the categories, Kant also provides a transcendental deduction or justification; as otherwise, he remarks, we could only use them 'dogmatically,' *i.e.* without any warrant at all—the procedure for which he blamed the Wolffian rationalists.

But the transcendental deduction of the Ideas of the reason differs widely, he held, from that of the categories of the understanding[4]. Perhaps we may find, on a closer

---

[1] *Encyclopaedie*, iii. p. 151.

[2] Except in admitting 'the anthropocentric standpoint' of our spatial intuition (A. pp. 26 f. = B. pp. 42 f.). Kant's early *penchant* for metageometrical speculation is an interesting topic which we must here pass over. Had he remembered it in his critical days, he might have been less confident in his transcendental exposition of space than he was.

[3] These correspond, it should be noticed, to the three divisions of the Wolffian Ontology—its so-called Rational psychology, Rational cosmology and Rational theology.

[4] Cf. the Appendix to the *Transcendental Dialectic*, A. pp. 669 ff. = B. pp. 697 ff.

comparison than Kant thought it worth while to make, that the difference is less than he supposed. In the first place he remarks that the objective validity of the categories is complete, since the experience we actually have would be impossible apart from the principles based upon them. By means of these principles our several experiences are articulated into that unity which we call Nature[1]. But this, he next remarks cannot be said of the Ideas of the reason: they are not essential to experience *as such*, inasmuch as they presuppose it while it does not presuppose them. Again, they are not 'ostensive,' do not set a definite object (*Gegenstand schlechthin*) before us: they are not, however, mere *entia rationis*, empty concepts without any object. On the contrary they have a certain content—just as the schematized category has—since they furnish the principles or maxims by means of which the empirical use of reason may attain, not indeed to more knowledge about objects, but to a systematic unity of that knowledge such as the understanding alone can never afford. In fact, they advance beyond the understanding as this advances beyond sense: they likewise limit the understanding as that limits sense. "Thus,"—at the end of his *Dialectic*—Kant concludes, "all human knowledge begins with intuitions, advances to concepts and ends with Ideas[2]." Surely a certain continuity is here implied: where the functions of the understanding must end the functions of the reason begin. But finally understanding and reason are alike in that both are only regulative *as regards the unity which they seek*[3]. In this respect the 'analogies' of the one correspond to the so-called 'maxims' of the other. The main difference

---

[1] Cf. A. p. 216 = B. p. 263.   [2] A. p. 702 = B. p. 730.
[3] A. p. 701 = B. p. 729 *fin.*

is that the latter 'prescribe (*gebieten*) greater unity than
the empirical use of the understanding can ever reach[1].'
Again we can only say: surely this is a difference of degree
rather than a difference of kind. So much continuity
between the functions of the understanding and those of
the reason seems then to lend a certain probability to the
supposition that the anthropomorphism which Kant recognised in the latter does in fact underlie the transcendental philosophy as a whole. But first it will be well to
examine somewhat fully such anthropomorphism as Kant
openly recognised.

In the case of rational cosmology the presence of an
antinomy hinders us from hypostasizing the universe,
Kant has said[2]. There are, however, no antinomies in
rational psychology or theology and so we are free so far
to be anthropomorphic here. Still there would obviously
be no point in calling the Ego or Subject of rational
psychology anthropomorphic: for this Subject is itself the
sole source from which all anthropomorphic comparisons
spring. As to the Idea of the self being just a kind of
substance—a soul—this is not anthropomorphic: it is
rather what it were better to call hylomorphic, if the term
may be allowed. Unfortunately Kant adheres consistently
to neither of these very different psychological ideas—if
'soul,' etymology notwithstanding, can be called a *psychological* idea[3]. As already said the faculty-psychology
dominant in his day tended to obscure his own supreme
principle—the centrality of the appercipient self—and led

[1] Cf. A. pp. 508 f. = B. pp. 537 f.
[2] A. p. 673 = B. p. 701. The case of a realm of ends for the practical
reason is, however, different.
[3] Cf. A. pp. 648 f. = B. pp. 676 f.; A. p. 672 = B. p. 700.

him to assimilate faculties to forces (*Kräfte*), and so to blend the idea of a soul or substance with that of the appercipient self[1]. However we shall have to deal with this question later on[2]. For the present we may safely take the 'personally identical self' as the true psychological 'Idea'; for after all it is Kant himself who says: "'I think' is the sole text of rational psychology[3]."

If then the Idea of rational psychology be that of a person, the anthropomorphism of the Idea of rational theology should consist in regarding God as if he were a person. And there are many passages in which Kant expressly so regards that Idea, but two of them may here suffice.

(1) At the end of a 'critique of all speculative theology' with which Kant closes the last part of his *Dialectic* the idea of God is described as 'that of a Supreme Being, the first ground (*Urgrund*) of all that exists, to which attributes pertain which we—judging from their consequents (*ihren Folgen nach*)—conceive as analogous to the dynamical realities of a thinking being, but as liable to none of the limitations which sense unavoidably imposes on the intelligences we come through experience to know.' This 'flawless ideal' is, he declares, 'a conception which completes and crowns the whole of human knowledge[4].'

(2) Again in the important Appendix to the *Dialectic*

[1] A. p. 682 = B. p. 710.
[2] Cf. below, § 24. Meanwhile Professor Norman Smith's *Commentary to Kant*, 1918, pp. 473–7 may be consulted where the two passages first cited are given at length.
[3] A. p. 343 = B. p. 401.
[4] A. p. 641 = B. p. 689. In the original the argument leads to this statement taking the form of a double negation. It is here expressed affirmatively.

he concludes by saying: "We are then entitled not only
to regard the World-cause in idea...as a being which has
understanding, feels pleasure and displeasure, and accordingly has desires and a will, etc., but to attribute to it
infinite perfection, which therefore far surpasses any that
we could be entitled through our empirical knowledge of
the order of the world [to entertain]¹."

But in addition to this 'more subtle anthropomorphism,'
as he calls it, in which a certain *resemblance* between the
Supreme Being and ourselves is assumed², Kant has referred to a 'symbolic anthropomorphism' implying nothing
more than an *analogy*. Now there may be a perfect analogy
in the relation of one thing to another thing, which has no
resemblance to it whatever: so here. "All that I mean,"
says Kant, "is that as a watch to its designer, a ship to its
builder, a regiment to its commander so the phenomenal
world (or whatever immediately underlies it)—and of this
I am a part—is related to the Unknown as it is for me."
But then he proceeds at once to say "that involved in this
analogy there remains what is *for us* a sufficiently definite
concept of the Supreme Being. Though we can determine
nothing as to what that Being is absolutely and in itself,
yet we determine its relation to the world and so to ourselves. And this [symbolic anthropomorphism] remains
when all objective anthropomorphism is abandoned. Once
then it is allowed as a necessary hypothesis³ that there is
'a First Being (*Urwesen*) conceived under purely onto-

¹ A. p. 700 = B. p. 728.
² "And without this," he parenthetically remarks, "we can think nothing
about it."
³ But, it has been objected, Kant has himself debarred reason from using
transcendental hypotheses in its speculations (A. pp. 773 f.=B. pp. 801 f.).
'Necessary *hypo*thesis,' however, is strictly speaking a contradiction in

logical predicates, substance, cause, etc.'—and this the deistic position, must be allowed; and it can be, since the use of pure categories entails no anthropomorphism— there is nothing to hinder us from predicating of this Being a *causality through reason*, and so advancing to theism. And the only possible way of thoroughly and consistently pursuing to the uttermost the application of reason to all possible experience in the phenomenal world is to assume a Supreme Reason as a cause of all connexions in the world[1]." In a word deism implies only a Supreme Thing *per se*, but theism, for which it opens the way, assumes a Supreme Reason, which implies a living God, and surely that is to say again a personal God. Kant's 'flawless ideal' then was that of a resemblance between the divine and the human personality. We have however, no means of theoretically knowing the Being himself to which this Idea points, 'cannot by searching find out God.'

When, however, we turn to reason on its practical side, and this for Kant was its primary side, we find ourselves in possession of new categories concerning what ought to be, and these yield a new clue to what is. Here the mere Idea of theoretical reason becomes for practical reason a reality which it must *postulate* if the moral order of the world is to stand[2]. But a postulate essential to the realisation of what we ought to be, yet based not on what we know but on what we are, is surely nothing if it is not

terms; and is here but one of many instances of Kant's careless terminology. What he seems to have in mind is simply that phenomenon *ex vi termini*, implies a thing *per se* that appears—a position which he never questioned.

[1] *Prolegomena*, §§ 57, 58, pp. 175–8, condensed and freely rendered.
[2] Cf. *Critique*: 'Of the Canon of Pure Reason,' ch. ii.

anthropomorphic, that is to say analogical in the sense of Kant's theoretic ideal. So much then for the avowed anthropomorphism of Kant's first two *Critiques*.

§ 14. The Critique of the Judgment

The third, that of the so-called faculty of Judgment (*Urtheilskraft*) which is supposed to mediate between and to complete the other two is especially important, as people are beginning at length to see[1]. Here again from first to last anthropomorphism, though not openly acknowledged, is nevertheless involved in the two loosely connected critiques of which it is composed, the one dealing with aesthetics, the other with biology. To this then let us now turn.

First of all we must be clear as to what Kant meant by *Urtheilskraft* or 'power of judgment.' Originally he meant what we call sagacity or judiciousness, the faculty of diagnosing whether a case in question is 'to be subsumed under a given rule or not, is or is not *casus datae legis*.' Its general function, in short, was to decide what minor premisses are appropriate to a given major premiss. To guard it here against mistakes (*lapsus judicii*) formal logic is obviously of no avail; for that takes no account of content. It is otherwise, however, with transcendental logic; for this does. Here we have the categories and the principles based on them: these, as *a priori* and so far independent of experience, instruct the judgment in applying the concepts of the understanding to phenomena[2]. So far

---

[1] Already Fichte and Schelling had hailed it as '*das Geistreichste und Bedeutungsvollste der drei Hauptwerke Kant's.*' Harms, *Die Philosophie seit Kant*, 1876, pp. 251, 256.

[2] A. pp. 132 f. = B. pp. 171 f. This introductory exposition of his

as it merely subsumes particulars under the universal laws already provided by the understanding, the judgment has no need of a law of its own to direct it: it is *ipso facto* '*determinant*' in virtue of those. They do not, however, enable it to subsume the innumerable diversities in the particulars that nature presents, under what Bacon called *axiomata media*. These 'axiomata' being only empirical, are not prescribed *a priori*; they have, in fact, to be found. Still, if they are to be laws, they must imply some principle somewhere to guide the ascent of the judgment to them from the said bewildering manifold of particulars. Such principle the judgment cannot borrow from experience; for precisely what it has itself to do (*die Obliegenheit hat*) is to establish 'the unity of all empirical principles under higher but likewise empirical principles, and so to render their systematic specification and continuity (*Unterordnung*) possible.' Such a 'transcendental principle'—since the guidance of understanding is not here available—the judgment then can only prescribe to itself: thus it is that it becomes what Kant called *reflective*.

The reflexion, which at this juncture arises, is briefly this: As the general laws of nature have their ground in *our* understanding which prescribes them to nature; so special empirical laws might be regarded as if they in like manner were prescribed by an understanding (though *not*

analytic of principles only shews the needless difficulties in which Kant's thoroughly artificial 'architectonic' entangled him. In the *Prolegomena* this intervention of a faculty of judgment is chiefly conspicuous by its absence. In the summary given in the preface to the *Metaphysische Anfangsgründe u.s.w.* it is not mentioned (*Werke,* IV. p. 384 *n.*); nor again in the later and fuller summary, *Fortschritte u.s.w.* 1791 or later. (Cf. Norman Smith's *Commentary,* pp. 332 f.) However, the *application* made of his exposition in the third *Critique* is all that immediately concerns us.

principle of purposiveness (*Zweckmässigkeit*). It does not, however, entitle the judgment to ascribe purposes (*Zwecke*) to nature. This only 'an intuitive understanding' might entitle it to do, but ours does not; for End (τέλος), unlike Substance and Cause, is not, according to Kant, a category of our understanding. This principle then is merely regulative for the reflective judgment: it is not constitutive of things: in other words, it has only subjective, not objective, validity.

There is a terrible lack of historical sense in this arbitrary and wholly imaginary description of a quandary that certainly never actually arose. Moreover, faculty-psychology of the worst sort runs riot through the whole of it. But, leaving aside all this artificiality, the one obvious point which at once strikes us is that this *assumption* of an understanding distinct from ours yet conforming to our needs is a clear case of anthropomorphism. And the more Kant insists—as he does again and again and again—that this indispensable 'principle,' which the judgment in its extremity prescribes to itself, is only regulative for it and not constitutive in respect of nature's products, the more obvious its anthropomorphism becomes. Solely on this account has it seemed needful to dwell on this so-called 'transcendental principle' of judgment as 'reflective.' It is, in fact, regarded on its epistemological side nothing but the postulate of the uniformity of nature on which all inference by induction or analogy depends, a postulate which is rooted anthropologically in our 'primitive credulity.' All such inference Kant himself has expressly declared is never more than 'presumptive,' not apodeictic, yielding therefore no universal, but only empirical, propositions. Hence it calls for caution and sagacity in its employment[1]. In so saying Kant recalls to us his original identification of judgment with mother-wit, common sense or judiciousness[2]. Again in a passage in the Appendix to the *Dialectic* of the *Critique of Pure Reason*, just now referred to, all the faults of subreption or false subsumption there disclosed he attributes entirely to lack of judgment[3]. All these points Kant seems here to have forgotten in accrediting judgment with a transcendental principle. It is further noteworthy that in neither of the two parts of this *Critique* is any effective use made of this supposed transcendental function of the reflective judgment to 'subsume under rules[4].'

It is otherwise, however, with the function of the reflective judgment regarded as a *facultas dijudicandi* or *Beurtheilungsvermögen*[5]; this then we may next consider. The first or aesthetical part of this *Critique* is mainly concerned with reflective judgment in this sense, *i.e.* not with primary predications (*Urtheilen*), but with certain secondary predications, judgments about judgments, as it has been said—in other words with estimations (*Beurtheilungen*). Of this kind are all reflective judgments in which the predicates pleasant, beautiful, useful, good (or their contraries) occur. These all presuppose determinate existence of *some sort*[6], and all assert value, positive or negative. As we say nowadays, they are appreciations not descriptions.

[1] *Logik. Werke*, VIII. pp. 128 f. Kant is here entirely at one with Locke: both indeed make use of the same term 'presumption.' Cf. Locke's *Essay*, IV. xiv. 4.

[2] Cf. above, p. 94.   [3] Cf. A. p. 643 = B. p. 671.

[4] Obviously this description is quite inappropriate to a process which consists not in submitting to rules but in seeking them.

[5] Cf. *Werke*, VI. pp. 381 f.

[6] Not necessarily actual existence: it is sufficient if 'the beautiful thing,' for example, is present in idea.

Such appreciations are implicit in all experience. Primarily and essentially they have then always a subjective reference. They are however explicit only at the self-conscious level, since it is here first that reflexion is possible; but then some may prove to be 'objective' in the sense of being universally valid.

Now different persons, even when they agree in describing an object, often disagree entirely so soon as they proceed to an appreciation of it (Kant's *Beurtheilen*). Such divergence is sometimes explicable by taking account of 'circumstances': these may make an object useful to one person which is useless to another. Sometimes divergence is attributable to differences in idiosyncrasy, which, as we say, makes one man's food another man's poison. Individual divergences of this sort—especially the latter —we may call idiomorphic. But if there are reflective judgments in which—though their ground is still purely subjective—all by common consent agree, we may surely call these anthropomorphic. Such a distinction, so Kant maintained, divided judgments concerning the agreeable or the useful from judgments concerning the beautiful or the good. The former, he held, were merely 'private' or, as we may say, idiomorphic: the latter were *a priori* or, as we may say in this case, anthropomorphic. We need not stay to discuss whether this sharp distinction is, in fact, ever as applicable as Kant supposed[1], or whether it is consistent with his own admissions, *e.g.* concerning want of taste, bad taste, the culture of taste, *etc.*[2]; for the main

[1] Considerations to the contrary are advanced by Lotze. Cf. his *Geschichte der Aesthetik in Deutschland*, 1868, pp. 250 ff. Cf. also W. M. Urban, *Valuation: Its Nature and Laws*, 1909, p. 205.
[2] Cf. *e.g.* § 32.

point is that in *any case the purely subjective reference is common to them all.* All estimation, all preference, presupposes feeling; and therefore, in characterizing objects from this standpoint, whether we agree or whether we differ, we are all equally applying a subjective standard, and so far are all alike anthropomorphic or at least 'anthropometric' in Protagoras's sense of the word. Here at length we come upon what was really the germinal idea of this, Kant's final *Critique, viz.* the fact of feeling. It will help us forward first of all to trace its evolution from this standpoint.

§ 15. *The Æsthetical Judgment*

Kant was confident that he had already ascertained the *a priori* principles of cognition, the first, and of volition, the last, in order of our fundamental faculties. But for feeling—which in fact, *i.e. empirically,* connects these faculties together—he had hitherto held that no *a priori* principle could be found. Yet this position, supposed to be psychologically incontrovertible, he was now at last led to question. For now, with his two earlier critiques completed before him, he came to realise that an 'immeasurable gulf' lay between their two domains, the sensible world, which is all that we can know, and the supersensible world, to which as moral agents we belong. In the one the concept of nature is supreme, in the other the concept of freedom; but these, as such, have nothing in common. Yet they can and must have a ground of connexion; for whatever *ought to be,* according to the moral law, must be possible in accordance with the laws of nature. And, in fact, when we speak of 'a gulf' this does not mean that, because they

have no common boundary, there is actually any intermediate region between them—a sort of buffer state, as
we say nowadays—separating the realm of nature from
the realm of ends. The gulf consists simply in the inac-
cessibility to any possible *knowledge* of ours of the higher
dimensions, so to say, of 'the one illimitable field of things
per se.' This underlies the entire sensible or phenomenal
world to which our experience and all our overt acts are
exclusively confined. But it was still possible, Kant
thought, to discover some *a priori* principle which for us
—who belong to both realms, though we have knowledge
only of one—may connect the laws of the one realm, which
we ought to obey, with the laws of the other, in which we
actually live and move. Such principle can in itself be
neither a principle of knowledge nor a principle of conduct; since it could then no longer serve as a connecting
link between the two, that is to say between the causality
of nature and the causality of freedom. To find this
principle was the new problem that now led Kant to
reconsider the 'criticism of feeling[1].'

Incontrovertible, as regards pleasure and displeasure in
general, he still admitted his old psychological position to
be. But there was after all one exception, the feelings
called aesthetic *par excellence*. These add nothing to knowledge, and so are distinct from the forms of sense-intuition
expounded under the title of *Aesthetik* in the first *Critique*.
Further—so at least he supposed—they are entirely disinterested, and therefore do not concern the conative
faculty, the topic of the second[2]. Here then were two

---

[1] Cf. Introduction, §§ ii and ix.

[2] But, as Kant has himself admitted, there may be interest without
conation. Such 'immediate interest' is characteristic of the aesthetic attitude.
"Taste for the beautiful is alone a disinterested and *free* satisfaction."

statements applicable to no other feelings. So perhaps
after all Baumgarten was not 'mistaken in his attempt to
bring the critical estimation (*Beurtheilung*) of the beautiful
under principles of reason,' as Kant had hitherto maintained[1]. Accordingly, no sooner had he completed the
new edition of his *Critique of Pure Reason* and got his
Critique of Practical Reason ready for press than he set
about preparing the groundwork for a third, which was
to be entitled *Rudiments of the Critique of Taste*[2]. This
preliminary essay, however, never appeared; for his insight
had grown apace, so that six months later he reported that
the *Critique* itself was nearly ready[3]. The '*Systematik*'
which had served him so well before, had now—he relates
in an emotional outburst—enabled him to discover *a
priori* principles for feeling too, and so to recognise a
third domain of philosophy besides the theoretical and the
practical, *viz.* the teleological! This discovery dawned
upon him, filling him with wonder, as soon as he noticed
the parallel in the position of feeling, midway between
cognition generally and conation, and the position of
judgment, midway between the understanding and reason.
Since the understanding provided the *a priori* principles

---

1 Cf. A. p. 21 *n.* = B. p. 35 *n.* The latter, it has been often pointed out,
shews signs of the impending misgiving. B. was published in 1787 and the
present *Critique* in 1790.

2 *Letter to Schütz*, June 1787, *Werke*, VIII. pp. 735 f.

3 *Letter to Reinhold*, Dec. 1787, VIII. pp. 739 f. Writing again to Reinhold in March '88 he expected to publish this *Critique of Taste* that
autumn (*loc. cit.* p. 741 *fin.*); but in a third letter fourteen months later he
looked to have it out by Michaelmas '89 with the new title, *Critique of
Judgment*, that it now bears, of which, he remarks, "the Critique of Taste
is only a part." It actually appeared six months later still, *i.e.* at Easter 1790,
and then hurriedly and very imperfectly revised. Perhaps its enlarged scope
was one cause of the delay.

of knowledge and the reason (which is constitutive so far as it is practical), the *a priori* principles of conduct, what more natural than to suppose the judgment to provide *a priori* principles for feeling[1]? More especially as without this *assumption*—though the empirical connexion of feeling with cognition on the one hand and with conation on the other, is evident enough—'our mind (*Gemüth*) would be only an aggregate of powers and not a 'system[2].' The functional continuity of cognition, feeling and conation, he here—as often—ignores. Cognition, feeling, and conation are never an aggregate, and never exist apart. It was, however, only in the one case of aesthetic feeling that he fancied he had discovered in the empirical facts of feeling an *a priori* concept that bridged the gulf between the concept of nature as the realm of law and the concept of freedom in the realm of ends. All this is doubtless as wonderful for us as it was for Kant; but for most of us probably the wonder is of a very different sort. Anyhow, so it seems to have been that Kant's afterthought about taste developed into this "*Critique of Judgment* as a means of connecting the two parts of philosophy into a whole[3]."

[1] The question thus generally stated would lead one to expect that the principles sought would apply to feeling as a whole, and not merely to the feeling which arises when we estimate (*beurtheilen*) certain objects as 'beautiful.' Surely this still leaves the serious gap between cognition and conation where it was. If aesthetic feeling is entirely disinterested, its exceptional character so far from providing any *a priori* principle connecting pure understanding and practical reason is just the one feeling least capable of connecting cognition and conation at all—a fact which the characterological study of 'aesthetic natures' amply confirms. This gap Kant might have made good, and probably would have done if he had been less intent on finding an *a priori* basis for æsthetics and kept a more open mind for fact. Cf. Adickes, *Kants Systematik u.s.w.* 1887, pp. 150 f.

[2] Cf. *Werke*, vi. pp. 380, 379.

[3] The title given to § iii of the Introduction.

The concept whereby this connexion is effected Kant called *Zweckmässigkeit*—a technical term of his which it is by no means easy to translate. Purposiveness by which it is commonly rendered would be retranslated *Absicht-lichkeit*. Adaptedness seems the only safe term when we need to be exact, and Kant himself frequently used its equivalent *Angemessenheit* and sometimes *Anpassung, i.e.* fitness. Teleology, as treating of final cause or end, no doubt presupposes adaptation; but the converse is not true; and in fact Kant describes aesthetic *Zweckmässigkeit* —with which this *Critique* is primarily concerned—as *Zweckmässigkeit ohne Zweck*, purposiveness without purpose and that implies only adaptation.

It was his analysis of aesthetic estimation which led him to maintain that this important concept has an *a priori* basis. The first question which he raised was whether in this case the feeling of pleasure precedes or follows the appreciation of the object as beautiful. "The solution of this question," he said, "is the key to the critique of taste[1]." If the feeling preceded, it would, as he maintained, be determined solely by the object itself as *given* and would —as we have seen—be as 'idiomorphic' as any other empirical feeling. This, however, is a supposition incompatible with the large amount of universality, which we must allow to be a characteristic of aesthetic judgment. But if the feeling presupposes the appreciation (*Beur-theilung*), on what exactly does that depend? We need not pause at this point to follow out Kant's analysis, encumbered as that is by his lumbering and superfluous array of faculties. The old commonplace, 'beauty is unity in variety,' as expounded by Francis Hutcheson, for example

[1] § 9; cf. § 35.

—to whom Kant owed more than he ever acknowledged —contains all the answer we want[1]. But why does unity in variety give us pleasure? Because, Kant replied, the mere contemplation of such 'form,' as he called it, evokes the free play of imagination controlled by understanding; the variety, which alone might bewilder, is grasped as a harmonious, or symmetrical, or rhythmical, or otherwise consentient, whole. Aesthetic pleasure, that is to say, is "the effect of the more facile interplay of both faculties as quickened by their mutual accord[2]." This is what he meant by the adaptedness (*Zweckmässigkeit*) of the Beautiful to our faculties. Further, because it is formal, this adaptation is, and he held must be, the same for everyone; since the same faculties are here exercised in the same way by us all. And so, though it is really subjective, we attribute this form to the object and call *that* beautiful. But from the standpoint of nature, to which the object belongs, there is no more meaning in this than in other of our subjective appreciations: what calls them forth is for nature purely contingent. There is adaptation to us but no corresponding design or end in it. Clearly then, the whole situation is anthropomorphic: it suggests spirit greeting spirit to *us*; and that is all we can say; and it is, in fact, upon this note that Kant himself concludes this part of his *Critique*[3].

What then has the supposed faculty of judgment to do with all this? Psychological reflexion brings to light this aesthetic 'form' with its subjective and yet universal or 'anthropomorphic 'character. We might call this reflexion

[1] Hutcheson's *Inquiry into the original of our ideas of Beauty and Virtue*, 1725, was translated into German in 1762.
[2] § 9 *fin*.
[3] Cf. § 58 on the Idealism of the æsthetic judgment and § 59 on Beauty as the symbol of Morality.

judgment; but who would dream of calling it a principle which prescribes or even postulates what it finds? No wonder Kant felt himself impelled at the end of his preface—when presumedly his *Critique* was finished—to own up to a 'perplexity' in treating of the aesthetic judgment in the first part, which he did not feel in dealing with the teleological judgment in the second. But he adds, 'it is precisely this riddle which necessitates' their separate treatment. There is no doubt that he considered the objects we appraise as beautiful to be subjectively teleological, that is to say, to be adapted to us—since they evoke the harmonious working of imagination and understanding—before he thought of connecting taste with judgment as reflective at all[1]. It was in so doing that he set himself the riddle which he could not afterwards satisfactorily solve. Again no doubt the omission of teleology from his philosophy left a fatal gap; but the obvious remedy— barred, however, for him by his beloved 'systematic'— was to recognise teleological and axiological categories. As it was, that Systematic, which he fancied had hitherto served him so well, once more 'embrangled him in inextricable difficulties,' to use a phrase of Berkeley's. For this he blamed not himself but the 'hardly avoidable obscurity' of his self-imposed problem—*viz.* to discover a cognitive faculty for feeling which should unite the sensible with the supersensible world. How it could be called a cognitive faculty, if it yielded no knowledge and could yield none was just the enigma which Kant felt to be so perplexing[2].

[1] Cf. p. 103.
[2] It is perhaps worth while for completeness sake to note briefly the main features of the *impasse* into which Kant was here driven. The sense of beauty was found to depend on the joint working of imagination and understanding. But this same co-operation he had previously found to

Kunst und Natur eines ist nur, Art and Nature are at bottom one: such was the impression which Goethe derived from this double *Critique* of Kant's. We can hardly suppose that it was a conviction of this sort which led Kant himself to treat of the aesthetic and the teleological judgment as parts of one whole; since their fundamental differences are what he emphasizes most. Thus, in the first place, he held, that with feeling, which is the key to the one, the other has nothing whatever to do. Again the aesthetic judgment he held yields not knowledge but

characterize all judgment, constituting, in fact, the difference between a mere association of two terms (the so-called 'judgment of perception') and the proposition (or judgment of experience) in which the copula expresses their objective unity for thought. (Cf. *Critique of Pure Reason*, B. § 19.) Judgment (*Urtheilen*) in this sense pertains entirely to the understanding: it yields a primary not a secondary judgment and the result is an item of knowledge. In the case of the aesthetic judgment or appreciation (*Beurtheilung*), however, the result is not an item of objective knowledge: it is a feeling. But Kant was not content with saying that the feeling *depends upon* the harmonious working of imagination and understanding: he insisted that it was due to the reflexion which discloses that fact. On the strength of that unwarrantable position he essays to bring the two forms in which imagination and understanding co-operate into line.

How now does Kant contrive to achieve this result? He plays fast and loose with the two inconsistent views of the understanding already mentioned (cf. above, p. 94 *n.* 2) as given in the first and second books of his *Analytic* respectively. In the latter the understanding is reduced to a faculty of concepts and the function of the judgment (*Urtheilskraft*) is in general to subsume appropriate cases under these. But feeling yields no objects to be subsumed under concepts. What then is there left for the aesthetic judgment to subsume? "Taste," Kant replies, "as subjective power of judgment (*Urtheilskraft*) involves a principle of subsumption, not however of intuitions under *concepts*, but of the *faculty* of intuitions or presentations (*Darstellungen*), *i.e.* the imagination, under the *faculty* of concepts, *i.e.* the understanding, so far as the former *in its freedom* accords with the latter in its *conformity to law*" (§ 35 *fin.*). But how can one independent faculty be 'subsumed' under another, and that by a third faculty in some respects independent of either, in others dependent on both? No commentator on Kant, so far as I know, has yet straightened out this coil.

appreciations and so connects the conative faculty with the cognitive; whereas the teleological judgment pertains entirely to the latter; and so, strictly speaking, it calls for no special critique at all. Lastly, an aesthetic judgment, he held, is immediate and it alone involves a principle claiming to be completely *a priori*; for it is concerned only with a form pertaining to the subject. A teleological judgment, on the other hand, turns on a form pertaining to the object; it is not immediate but requires many special experiences before its object can be even empirically determined; and it can adduce no principle from the concept of nature authorising it to ascribe to this *a priori* any reference to ends. In short, whereas the aesthetic judgment is a constitutive principle, the teleological judgment is only a regulative or heuristic principle, an 'allowable hypothesis' forced upon us by the discursive character of our understanding[1]. The chief point they have in common is that reflective judgment is supposed to be concerned in both. But what if reflective judgment is only connected with 'the aesthetic sense' by the fanciful afterthought to which Kant was led by his 'Systematic'? This, in fact, seems the sole link between them—a link acknowledged, so far as I know, by no other thinker either before Kant or since. What the reflective judgment has to do with teleology we have still to see.

[1] Cf. on these differences Introduction § VIII, pp. 199 f., § IX, p. 203, § 58, p. 361, § 61, p. 371, § 73, p. 407, § 78, pp. 423, 427. Cf. also an article entitled *Ueber den Gebrauch teleologischer Principien in der Philosophie* written two years earlier, where Kant says roundly that in respect of nature the use of these principles is always empirical (*Werke*, IV. p. 494).

§ 16. *The Teleological Judgment*: (1) *the Analytic*, (*a*) *the Purposiveness of Nature*

It does not surprise us then to find, on coming to the second part of this *Critique of Judgment*, that its sole problem is entirely distinct from that of the preceding part; is in fact only that very ancient one concerning final causes. This term, as everyone knows, we owe to Aristotle, who again and again declared that "Nature makes nothing in vain," in other words, is always teleological. And Kant too—having enounced the principle of teleology to be that "an organized product of nature is one in which all is reciprocally end and means"—continues, repeating Aristotle's very words, "nothing in it is in vain, purposeless or attributable to a blind mechanism of nature[1]." Yet nature as 'blind mechanism' is all the nature that he began by recognising: concerning this and this only we have judgments that are at once determinant and entirely *a priori*. This, as we have seen, was the philosophy of nature analyzed in his first *Critique* and more fully expounded in the *Metaphysical Foundations of the Natural Sciences*. The law of inertia, that all the changes in nature have an external cause is here declared to be fundamental in any science of nature strictly so called. Final causes on the contrary are always due to 'internal causes': to include them in nature would 'be the death of all natural philosophy.' A hard and fast line then separates the two: in a word, 'an organized product of nature,' regarded as objective, is a flagrant contradiction, that is to say if nature is simply mechanical.

An 'internal cause' for Kant implied life or mind. "We

[1] § 66 *init.*

know," he says, "of no other internal principle of a substance to change its state....If we seek the cause of a material change in life, we shall have at once to seek it in another substance distinct from matter, yet connected with it[1]." The external, inanimate, world then is not 'all there is,' for it here presents itself as a means to the ends of another, the internal, animate world, which its own definition as 'external and inanimate' implies. Still means to our ends need not be ends of nature however widely we understand the term; and the bad teleology that arose from neglect of this distinction Kant has ruthlessly but effectively exposed[2]. It is not nature's powers or products as useful or beneficial *relatively* to man or other creatures that is Kant's problem. It is first, the *inner* purposiveness which man and his fellow creatures themselves display as living organisms; and then, the further problem to which this leads on, that of nature as a whole as possibly a system or realm of ends. It is only along with this further problem that the consideration of the external or relative adaptation of nature's products to each other is in place. Nevertheless it was this relative adaptation as involved in our own artifacts that led Aristotle to his classical doctrine of causes. Kant, of course, does not question the objective reality of artifacts, but so regarded they are only on a par

---

[1] *Metaphysische Anfangsgründe, u.s.w. Werke,* IV. p. 440.

[2] Still in § 67, which deals with the teleology of nature in general as a system of purposes, Kant is as fanciful as any Paley could wish. Cf. p. 392 and his remarks there as to vermin, which 'may be a wise appointment of nature' to promote cleanliness; or as to mosquitoes, *etc.* as 'so many goads' to savages 'to drain the marshes...and make their habitations more healthy; as to the tapeworm, supposed to be given...as a kind of set-off for some defect in the vital organs; as to disturbing dreams as remedial when the stomach is overloaded; and even in a sound state of health preventing sleep from becoming the 'complete extinction of life.'

with the products of blind mechanism—the same physical
laws are exemplified in both.

Yet in the present *Critique* he advances far beyond the
standpoint of the *Critique of the Pure Reason* and the *Prolegomena.* The occasion of this advance we have already
seen. The facts of feeling and conation had led him in
treating of the aesthetic judgment to r:̈ ʒe the connexion
of these two realms which he had hitherto dealt with too
much as if they were really isolated. At the outset he had
defined nature as 'all that is' in distinction from whatever
ought to be[1]. But he held that we have no rational, no
a priori knowledge, of that part of 'nature in this widest
sense' to which the 'internal causes' belong—although
it is through these causes alone that what ought to be
can be realised. Psychology (and biology), and therefore
teleology, were then but *Fremdlinge der Naturphilosophie*,
strangers beyond the pale of whatever is properly to be
called *pure* science.

Still it is from the standpoint of science so understood
that Kant opens his present *Critique*. A certain 'subjective
purposiveness in nature,' an adaptedness to us, we have
good grounds on transcendental principles to assume—
hence we talk of 'beautiful forms.' So much, at any rate,
he claims to have already shewn. But any objective teleology of nature is, he insists, neither certain *a priori* nor
empirically verifiable. The concept of end must then have
been surreptitiously 'conjured into the nature of things'
by a prescientific sophistry (*Vernünftelei*) more intent on
rendering nature intelligible (*begreiflich*) than on acquiring
a knowledge of it based on objective grounds[2]. Yet before

---

[1] Cf. on the 'Architectonic of Pure Reason,' *Kritik d. r. V.* A. p. 845 =
B. p. 873.   [2] § 61, p. 371.

we reach the close of this *Critique* we find Kant, not merely justifying what he began by calling sophistry, but actually insisting upon the subordination of the mechanical, which is all that we are supposed scientifically to know (*wissen*), to the teleological which certainly is all that we can be said to understand (*begreifen*). The first may tell us something about the *how*, but only the last can suggest anything of the *why* of this evolving world in which we live and move and have our being[1].

Those two questions, *how* and *why*, are entirely distinct: the first might be answered completely, as Laplace imagined, and never give rise to the second at all. Their respective standpoints are then on different levels, and as already said, it is only in this *Critique* that Kant treats systematically of the higher of these. Here he is continually referring 'to nature in the widest sense, to which indeed we ourselves belong' as contrasted with nature as material and merely mechanical, to which—though we are connected with it—we certainly do not belong. But the wider horizon of this higher level, as Kant in his introductory section somewhat naively remarks, brings '*at least one principle more*' to bear on our investigation of nature, a new 'analogy' for reducing those of its phenomena to rules, for which the old analogies, as furnishing laws of simply mechanical causality, do not suffice. Such outstanding phenomena are artifacts and organisms.

With these as the empirical 'phenomena' which are

[1] No wonder then that philosophical interest in Kant's whole critical undertaking was in his own time and is now again in ours centered round this one—in which, as he states in the preface, his 'entire critical enterprise is completed.' Cf. above, p. 94 *n*. 1; also Windelband, *Geschichte d. neueren Philosophie*, 4te Aufl. (1907), p. 178, and B. Bauch, *Immanuel Kant*, 1917, *Vorwort*.

supposed to give rise to a special, the teleological, judgment Kant's *Analytic* of this judgment begins[1]. Artifacts he observes, we can understand, for they are our handiwork; but as to organisms, there we have no such insight; for to produce these artificially infinitely surpasses any art of ours. Moreover we observe certain differences between the two which point to an essential difference in the mode of their production. In making a chair, for example, we first shape its several parts, then afterwards we fit and join them together, and so, at last, the chair is there as a whole. In an organism, on the other hand, the whole comes first, and the parts are gradually differentiated within this. Further, in a watch say, one part is, no doubt, for the sake of the others, but it does not exist by their means; nor does a watch maintain, repair or reproduce itself. Above all, it is just 'driven' by a blind motive power: in a word, it is a mere machine. An organism, however, selects and recombines its own materials, and only as thus transformed and made plastic are they shaped into a consentient whole. An organism, in short, possesses a unique 'formative power' (*bildende Kraft*)[2] and is therefore *not* a mere machine. Finally, whereas a machine is produced piecemeal by an outside artificer, an organism is from the first an individual and one that generates (*erzeugt*) itself; provisionally then Kant would say, "it is, though in a double sense[3] *cause and effect* of itself." All these characteristics he illustrates by a biological description of the propagation, growth and development of a tree. *Inter*

---

[1] Cf. especially §§ 64 and 65.
[2] Later on Kant seemed to prefer to say 'formative impulse' (*Bildungstrieb*) as his correspondent Blumenbach had recently done. Cf. § 81, p. 438.
[3] That is to say phylogenetically and ontogenetically.

alia he more or less clearly foreshadows the anabolic and
katabolic processes—as they are called nowadays—which
all life involves on its physical side. "We say," then, he
concludes, "far too little of nature and its power in producing organisms (*Vermögen in organisierten Producten*) if
we employ the *analogon of art*."

He then resumes: "Perhaps we approach nearer
[nearer, that is, than in 'the distant analogy' of our own
artifacts] to this inexplorable property [of self-organiza-
tion] if we regard it as an *analogon of life*." How came he
to say '*perhaps* a nearer analogon'? The problem perplexed
him. For, he proceeded to argue: We must either endow
mere matter with a property essentially incompatible with
it (hylozoism) or assume an alien principle (a soul) associated
with it (interaction); to do either would be to remove the
product from nature as corporeal altogether. But difficulties
are no reason for ignoring facts; though it be true, as Kant
concludes by saying: "The organization of nature has then
nothing in it analogous to any causality that we know"—
true and trite if by nature we mean inanimate nature[1].
And surely organisms are not merely analogous to living
things: they are in fact alive. In this fact consists their
essential difference from artifacts. In this fact we have
the 'one principle more' that the wider survey of nature,
on which Kant now embarks, forced him at length to
take into account. And in this fact at the very outset he
incidentally recognises that subordination of mechanism
to life, on which, we shall find—as I have already said
—he comes in the end emphatically to insist. Obviously,
if life itself is the fact with which the teleology of nature
has to deal, it is utterly inept to set out by treating of it

---

[1] Cf. Herbart's strictures on this—*Metaphysik*, i. p. 135.

on the basis of a 'distant analogy' with human activity in making chairs and watches.

Yet this is what after all Kant continues to do, starting, as he does, from the body, 'inner *form*,' and not from the being (*Wesen*) whose 'formative impulse' is the initiating *function* which that form presupposes[1]. He distinguishes a moving or working cause which entails the transference of energy (*nexus effectivus*) from a final cause which is directed by an idea (*nexus finalis*). The one he calls *real*, the other *ideal*; for these terms, he fancies, enable us to see that the said two kinds of cause are all there are. They may, however, be more truly said to enable us to see, that if by cause (*Ur-sache*) we mean a *thing*, then things, *i.e.* 'substances' make up the only kind of efficient cause there is. An idea which only represents the effect to be attained cannot by itself suffice for the actual attainment; for in that case if "wishes were horses, beggars might ride." *All actual causes then are substantial causes*[2].

But these real causes we have seen Kant distinguishing by a more logical disjunction and a far more fundamental one, *viz.* as external or internal, *i.e.* as matter or mind[3]. The one is inert, the other is conative: matter does not move of itself, whereas mind may be said to do so. This spontaneity, as he sometimes called it, is what conation implies. And, in fact, we frequently find Kant, regardless

---

[1] Thus (in § 72, p. 403) he represents the problem of teleology as arising for us only in cases where the objective grounds are too deeply hidden for our investigation on the lines of mechanism; then, he remarks, "we make trial of a subjective principle, *viz. that of art, that is causality by way of* (*nach*) *ideas.*" Italics mine.

As to the precedence given to structure and 'inner form,' cf. § 65, p. 385 *init.*, § 65, p. 389, § 67, pp. 390 *fin.*, 391 *init.*

[2] Cf. above, p. 84.   [3] Cf. above, p. 110 *fin.*

of all that he has said of ideas and concepts as final causes, clearly enunciating the truth that the cause of a purposive action is always real, always a subject possessed of appetition or will. For instance, in a note to the preface of his *Critique of Practical Reason* there is the following: "Life is the capability of a being (*Wesen*) to act (*handeln*) according to conative laws. Conation is its capability *by means of* [*i.e.* guided by] its *presentations to be the cause* whereby the actuality (*Wirklichkeit*) of the objects of *these presentations* [is brought about]." In a further note in the present *Critique* referring to this passage he recognises the fact that a mere wish, the 'idea alone,' is futile; as, for example, when the subject is aware that his resources are insufficient to effect the realisation of the wished-for object[1]. *Internal causes then are not ideas but living agents.*

All living agents, however, are not on the same level: only in their upper ranks is there even a gleam of the intelligence which foresight and conscious selection of means to ends require. The earliest conations are impulsive, not deliberative: they do not depend on knowledge or ideas, though they may eventually lead to them. They are already 'internal' actions, but they are not yet in themselves purposeful or teleological. The psychologist may describe them as such in view of their ultimate result when—after much trial and error—they eventually succeed; but to attribute his own standpoint to a merely sentient subject would be a flagrant instance of 'the psychologist's fallacy'; and of this Kant here seems

---

[1] *Kritik d. pr. V. Werke*, v. p. 9 *n*. (italics Kant's own); the present *Critique*, *Einl.* § 3, p. 184 *n*. Cf. also § 10, p. 225, and § 64, p. 382, where will is described as the faculty of acting for ends (*das Vermögen nach Zwecken zu handeln*).

guilty[1]. A remark may here be interposed *à propos* of Kant's statement concerning the ontogeny of organisms, *viz.* that they develop (*erzeugen*) themselves. It is obvious that this also is not a case of conscious purpose, of an end attained under the guidance of ideas present to the living *being* (*Wesen*) itself. For all that, it implies not merely moving forces but a selective impulse (*Bildungstrieb*) which converts them into formative forces. The *modus operandi* here may be for ever inscrutable—if we restrict the meaning of Nature as Kant here does; but that is no reason for attempting to range it under the same category as artifacts, with which it has only 'a distant analogy[2],' when the more fundamental category of life is seen to be more appropriate, and to be, moreover, implied in both.

And it was assuredly not the analogy of art which first led advancing experience to recognise certain objects as 'ejects,' *i.e.* as other selves; nor is that analogy our 'clue' —to use Kant's term—now. It is not by resemblance in structure but by a certain identity of function that we recognise other selves. Though they have certainly no consciousness of any experience except their own, nevertheless the similarity in the behaviour of others to the way in which they behave themselves leads even creatures far below us to recognise at least their kind. The more varied and distinct the characteristics of what we take to be behaviour, the more confidently we assume the presence of individuality and life. It is behaviour then (or the semblance of behaviour) that is the ground of the distinction of ejects from mere objects. Such 'animatism' or anthro-

---

[1] Schopenhauer knew better and saw further. Cf. his *Werke*, 3te Ausg. (1873), III. pp. 373, 402.

[2] Cf. § 65, last paragraph but one.

pomorphism was too exuberant to have any clear limits at the first. Increasing intelligence, however, entailed its steady restriction. And, since the time of Descartes at any rate, that 'objective' side of nature has become sharply defined from which now Kant essays to start: the side described by negative terms such as inanimate, incapable, and inert, and therefore, in short, purposeless: its only positive characteristic being routine or uniformity as contrasted with initiative. Precisely on this account 'pure or exact,' albeit abstract, science is applicable to it; whereas of the other or ejective side of nature, to which our anthropomorphic interpretation still pertains, no such science is or ever will be possible. So we have the Cartesian dualism of matter and mind as well as the familiar opposition of science and history. It is this opposition fundamentally, that Kant in the present *Critique* at first essays to resolve from the wrong side; not from the side that still remains akin, but from the side which now *appears* to be alien, to us as selves.

But does not a more 'synoptic view' of the world as a whole suggest, that there is, in reality, no incongruity or incompatibility between the stable uniformity of 'the stage' and its 'properties' on the one hand and the everchanging drama of life and history that is there enacted on the other? Both, if they are verily two, are essential, but the latter alone gives meaning to the whole—a meaning which, as already said, could never be even conjectured from the completest knowledge of the former. Hence Kant was misled into speaking of the two as foreign (*fremdartig*), as if the world were sundered into 'heterogeneous' halves, which could never become a whole at all[1].

[1] This topic, to which we must presently return, is admirably unfolded

All these points and problems, we seem justified in saying—at any rate if we read between the lines—are either stated or implied in the empirical part of Kant's *Analytic*, which we have just considered. The one principle more, that nature as mechanism will not explain, is life. Self-conservation as the first law of life is the 'clue' which philosophers have frequently proclaimed, and which the biologist commonly postulates as unreservedly as he does the persistence of matter and energy. And Kant himself as good as says, that biologists can divest themselves of the one and the teleology which it implies, as little as they can of the other and the rigid concatenation of physical mechanism, which this in turn implies[1]. Now both, on his own shewing, are objective, that is to say real; for the one pertains to the internal, and the other to the external, causes which together constitute nature in the sense of 'all that is.' But for the external causes he claims to have already 'deduced' *a priori* principles, which are essential to the possibility of experience. Essential they may be (as the stage and 'properties' for history) but not sufficient[2]: internal causes (the *dramatis personae*) are certainly indispensable, if, as we have said, the whole is to have any meaning. "Yet into the possibility of a causality of that sort [such as we observe everywhere in life and mind] we have no *a priori* insight at all." With these words Kant concludes this first part of his *Analytic*[3].

by the late Wilhelm Dilthey in his *Einleitung in die Geisteswissenschaften*, 1883. Cf. pp. 473 ff.

[1] Cf. § 66, p. 389 *init.* Their salient difference Kant neglects to note. Cf. above, pp. 116 f.

[2] The supposed antinomy of the judgment, to which we shall have to refer presently, owes all its superficial plausibility to overlooking this simple difference between essential and sufficient—a fatal defect which von Hartmann has already exposed. Cf. his *Kant's Erkenntnistheorie und Metaphysik*, 1894, pp. 246–8.   [3] Cf. § 65, p. 388.

§ 17. *Analytic, (b) the Principle of Teleology*

Yet, inasmuch as this internal purposiveness though empirically ascertained, is also regarded by us as universal and necessary, it too must have 'some *a priori* principle or other (*irgend ein*) as its ground.' With this remark the second or transcendental part of the *Analytic* begins[1]. But if internal causes are here ultimate and so inexplicable facts, and if external causes are likewise ultimate and so far equally inexplicable, why must some further ground or other still remain to be found for the former, though none is required for the latter? Such ground obviously cannot in either case be a further fact; that is to say, it cannot on the empirical plane of our present inquiry be a *ratio essendi*: it is then a *ratio cognoscendi*. In other words the problem of this second part of the *Analytic* is epistemological. Even so, if in both cases we are concerned with efficient causes, why, we again ask, must 'some further ground or other' be still to seek in order to validate the knowledge we are assumed to have of all phenomena in which internal causes are involved? Because "into the possibility of a causality of that sort we have no *a priori* insight at all," Kant has told us.

At this point he brings forward again his psychological doctrine of a twofold function of the faculty of judgment[2]. There is no epistemological problem in the case of external causes because here determinant judgments are possible: in the case of internal causes that is impossible; and so there we have only the reflective judgment to help

---

[1] §§ 66–8.

[2] The case of the so-called aesthetic judgment, as we have already seen, is entirely different.

us. Now the determinant judgment subsumes under the *a priori* laws of the understanding which are based directly on the table of categories, laws already prescribed and '*ready to its hand*': in Kantian phrase, this judgment is '*constitutive.*' But the reflective judgment, having to deal with what is empirical and for us contingent, has no laws ready to its hand: therefore it cannot, in fact, begin by subsuming at all. It has first to assume that there *are* laws; and then by induction and analogy, which never yield more than presumptive evidence, it begins to seek them. Here organisms are the empirical facts with which it has to deal; and the epistemological problem is to render their possibility conceivable. Its procedure is only problematic, and if it succeeds the solution will only be '*regulative.*'

Here we may remark first of all that the problem raised turns entirely on the assumed completeness of Kant's table of categories, and this we have already found every reason to distrust—to say the very least[1]. As he himself most distinctly says: "If we were to ascribe to nature causes working *in a purposelike way* (*absichtlich*), so making teleology…a *constitutive* principle…then the concept of a natural purpose would no more [be anything] for the reflective, but would belong to the determinant, judgment[2]." It surely strikes us now as strange to treat as a mere supposition—and one, moreover, to be straightway rejected—a fact which we do not *ascribe* to nature, but which, taking nature to mean the entire sum of things, we actually find there from the first, and which to the last we understand best. And where in the world is there any warrant for its rejection except (in consequence of his

---

[1] Cf. above, pp. 44 f.   [2] § 61, p. 372 *fin*. Italics Kant's.

mechanical view of nature) the absence of teleological principles from Kant's programme? Yet, not only has he recognised this fact in talking—as we have seen—of 'internal causes'; but—so hard was it for him to expel—that, in the very act of explaining away its seeming objectivity, he is continually appealing to it as really objective[1].

Again, if the procedure in reflective judgment is at best only problematic and presumptive, how can it provide itself with an *a priori* ground whereby the possibility of organisms is rendered conceivable? If, on the other hand the relation of means and end were a category like the relation of cause and effect[2], teleology in short, only as with Aristotle a special case of aetiology, there would be no difficulty[3]. Teleology would be—on Kant's lines—also an *a priori* principle and one, as he rightly held, connecting theoretical and practical philosophy into a whole. That way out, however, Kant had—all unawares—barred against him by this very doctrine of reflective judgment,

---

[1] Here are some instances from this second part of the *Analytic*: "By the *example* that Nature *gives us* in her organic products we are justified, nay, called upon to expect of her and her laws nothing but what is purposive on the whole" (§ 67, p. 391). Again (p. 393): "If we have once *discovered* in Nature a capability (*Vermögen*) of bringing forth products that we can only think of 'teleologically' we go further still." This further advance, however, it is pointed out, carries us beyond knowledge to speculation, beyond the concept of organisms as natural products to an Idea of reason concerning the cause and end of nature as a whole. But (in § 68, p. 394), speaking of natural science, Kant remarks that "we must [here] scrupulously and humbly confine ourselves to the expression which *asserts exactly as much as we know*, namely a purpose (*Zweck*) of nature." Italics mine.
As to the *prima facie* objectivity which Kant allowed, cf. § 77 *init.*

[2] Which also, we may remark by the way, only emerged as the result of arduous reflexion. Cf. above, pp. 55 f. and 71 f.

[3] Causality has its problems, no doubt, but these do not here concern us.

by which he imagined he had effected one. That he was
not without misgivings and in some perplexity seems
fairly clear from the phrase 'some principle or other,'
which he has used not only in this place but also in his
preface, when referring 'to the great difficulties of finding
an *a priori* principle peculiar to the faculty of judgment.'
It is easy, he remarks, 'to gather from the nature of the
judgment' that such difficulties must exist[1]. Assuredly it
must be, if the reflective judgment alone—to say nothing
of the determinant—turns, first, as aesthetic, on the subjective capacity of feeling; secondly, as logical, on the
formal 'technique' of the law of specification, and thirdly
here, as objective, on the conceivability of organisms as
natural products. Neither feeling nor logic can be here of
any avail.

True and so much Kant allows: the teleological judgment turns neither on feeling nor on specification. Though
Kant still employs the vague term purposiveness (*Zweckmässigkeit*) which sufficed for them, it is now meant
definitely to imply purpose or end (*Zweck*). This new idea
of finality or internal causation the teleological judgment
uses; it uses it however only as an analogy. But before
using it in this fashion, it must first have come into
possession of it. We naturally ask: how? We get no clear
answer to our question in the *Analytic*. This, however, is
followed in accordance with Kant's systematic by a
Dialectic—a very superficial and artificial performance.
Yet here we get some light.

[1] Preface, p. 175.

§ 18. *The Teleological Judgment: (2) the Dialectic, the Idea prescribed by Reason*

We learn, first of all, that the reflective judgment has, so to say, two strings to its bow. In its quest for empirical laws, the maxim which the understanding suggests may up to a certain point suffice; but when a further maxim turns out to be indispensable, *i.e.* in the case of life and mind, reason comes into play to provide it. But maxims from different faculties may easily seem to collide. Hence, in fact, a natural dialectic has emerged, which Kant now proceeds to discuss at length and to resolve. After disposing of systems which deal with the purposiveness of nature dogmatically, he devotes a whole section to shewing that this concept is merely critical[1]; and such is the maxim which reason prescribes to the reflective judgment. In both cases, then, the physical as well as the biological, the reflective judgment, so far from prescribing its own maxims, has these already and *independently* provided for it. The maxim which the understanding provides is essential to the possibility of any experience at all; but it does not extend beyond nature as blind mechanism, in which only matter and energy are concerned. The maxim which reason is said to prescribe is equally essential to the possibility of nature as a realm of ends to be attained and maintained. In short, there is really no antinomy; for the maxims that seem to collide turn out to relate to different aspects or domains of nature as all that is. "It is just as necessary," Kant concludes, "to think for it [nature in this widest sense] a particular kind of causality which does

---

[1] § 79.

judgment according to him—that some *a priori* principle or other seemed to Kant to be requisite for its justification. Such a justification the Idea of God would furnish completely, if it were objectively valid; for as Kant proceeds to remark: "We can form absolutely no notion of such a world [as ours] except by thinking a *designedly working* Supreme Cause of it." And again: "We cannot make the purposiveness (*Zweckmässigkeit*), which must underlie our knowledge of the possibility of many natural things,... intelligible save by representing them and the world as due to an intelligent cause (God)[1]." It was for Kant, at any rate, as we have already seen, "the flawless ideal which completes and crowns the whole of human knowledge[2]." But theoretically it is only an Idea and therefore in Kantian phrase only regulative not constitutive. Can this be called a justification?

§ 19. *Teleology and Theology*

Towards this Idea then teleology points, but it does no more than point. Though Kant spoke always with the greatest respect of the 'teleological argument' he nowhere for a moment allowed that it was adequate. If we think design (*das Absichtliche*) to be universal throughout nature, this may *suggest* the Idea of divine genius as its Author. Still to argue from the one Idea to the other would be a 'delusive circle'—a case of the fallacy of *diallelon*[3]. Moreover the objective reality of neither is given. How distinct the two Ideas actually were in Kant's mind is shewn by the different answers which he thought

[1] Cf. § 75, pp. 411 *fin.*, 412 *fin.* Italics Kant's.
[2] Cf. above, p. 91 *fin.*   [3] Cf. § 68, p. 394.

were possible when the question of the origin of the world is raised. There are after all, he remarked, instances enough of discordant purposes in the world to suggest many authors rather than one—as indeed was in older times commonly assumed: polytheism being older than theism. It was even possible, he thought, that a Supreme Cause might be determined to its action by a mere necessity of its being (comparable with the technical instincts of animals) without according to it any wisdom at all, much less the highest[1]. If we knew that the purposes in the world were not merely empirically conditioned, but that there was one final purpose and that absolutely good, then we might infer a single Supreme Being of the highest wisdom and perfect in every respect. Such knowledge, however, since it relates to the supersensible, nature as phenomenal obviously could never supply.

Teleology then does not furnish the justification of the Idea of a Supreme Intelligence; on which Idea, nevertheless, it is supposed to be grounded. And yet reason has, independently of all teleology, a practical justification for postulating the existence of such a Being—"a proof indeed which would still retain all its cogency if we came across no evidence or none but doubtful evidence for physico-teleology." What is this new 'proof which *supplies* the conviction' that is there lacking? It consists in what Kant called ethico-theology; and the ground on which that proof rests is human *freedom*. "It is very remarkable," he says, "...that this is the only one of all the Ideas of pure reason, whose object is a thing of fact (*Thatsache*), and must be reckoned among the *scibilia*[2]." So it is that reason

---

[1] § 85, pp. 453, 455.
[2] § 91, p. 483 and especially p. 489. Here Kant advances beyond the

reveals two facts concerning the supersensible—man, as *homo noumenon* a member, and *God as the Head* (*Oberhaupt*), of the Realm of Ends[1], whose final purpose in the world lies in man and rational beings akin to him. In the realm of nature we can discern no final purpose, and so no purpose at all, save as means to that higher realm. We can now see why a physico-theology can be ancillary, but cannot be adequate, to a complete teleology. On the other hand—and this is one of the most important and original positions in Kant's philosophy—we can also see why there cannot be what, in contradistinction to ethical theology, Kant called 'theological ethic'; "for laws which reason itself does not give and the observance of which it does not [itself] effect, as a pure practical faculty, could not be moral [laws][2]." In that very remarkable fact of freedom "we have then a principle capable of determining the idea of the supersensible within us, but through this of [determining] it also without us," as available knowledge (*zu möglichen Erkenntniss*) although only in respect of practice[3]. So Kant brings his last *Critique* to a conclusion.

What, however, for the moment concerns us is not the new outlook on morality and religion which he here opens up, but simply so much of it as is relevant to the question raised just now, the question: What exactly is that Idea which reason, according to Kant, is said to prescribe to the judgment as reflective? If physico-teleology is only 'a propaedeutic to theology proper' the Idea of the final

'negative' position of the first *Critique* (B. p. 586); as indeed he did in the second. Cf. *Kr. d. prakt. Vernunft. Werke*, v. p. 49 f. Abbott's transl. pp. 135 ff.

[1] Cf. *Grundlegung der Metaphysik der Sitten* (1784), *Werke*, IV. p. 282. Abbott's transl. p. 52.

[2] § 91, p. 499.   [3] § 91, p. 489.

purpose of the world cannot have been the clue, which reason, it was said, here intervened to provide. We have already noted that the whole inquiry arose on the empirical plane: particular forms were the occasion for reflexions that disclosed the insufficiency of mechanism as a clue in investigating even the simplest forms of organic life. The '*receptivity*' or liability of inanimate nature to contingencies—anomalies, that is to say, for which its exclusively external causes cannot account—points clearly to a fact beyond the possibilities of inert matter altogether: to wit, the spontaneity of internal causes, a fact which alone suffices to make the said forms conceivable; for spontaneity is a main characteristic of our own life. But now we have the inquiry concluding by adducing another fact, pre-eminently an internal cause, *viz.* the volitional freedom of self-conscious persons. Between these two facts—(1) the spontaneity of all forms of life as bent—by reflex action or by instinct—on self-conservation (*Selbsterhaltung*), and (2) the pursuit, at the higher level of rational conduct, of self-realisation (*Selbstentfaltung*)—we nowadays for the most part feel there must be some continuity; since both in turn have been, and indeed still are, manifested in the lives of all of us. If this be true, it is at any rate a truth that Kant failed to appreciate, basing teleology, as he did in the first case, not on these facts but on a distant analogy derived from them. In the second case, no doubt, his analogy is as sound as it is remarkable; for moral values, to which men in all ages have been independently led, are the one solid basis for the Idea of God. The Idea or clue, then, which reason directs us to follow, is to interpret the world in terms of ourselves: in other words to orientate the natural by reference to the spiritual.

and activity of the subject itself are analogically projected[1]. Here then too, though it is not avowed, the
anthropomorphic character of Kant's standpoint is, as I
have already urged, unmistakeable.

But before we can advance from the mere formulation
of those analogies to their application in experience, a
further clue or guiding thread is indispensable, and one
more general than those laid down in the analogies themselves. According to the third *Critique*, the reflective judgment, on which that application devolves, is forced to
assume a formal adaptation underlying the seeming contingency of the world as we directly perceive it, as if an
intelligence not our own had—so to say—tempered nature
to our discursive understanding. This again, is unmistakeably anthropomorphic[2]. But there is a still more
important point to notice here. For the question at once
occurs to us:—Will not the more general clue, which the
reflective judgment is said to provide for itself, in the end
outflank its supposed subservience to the pure understanding: in other words, will not the 'analogies of experience' said to determine nature as mechanism turn out
after all not to be (effectively or objectively) constitutive
but to be only (subjectively) regulative? Such at any rate,
as we have already seen, has proved to be the case. The
antinomy between mechanism and teleology in which the
reflective judgment was supposed to be involved, disap-
peared when it was discovered that, in respect of *both*, this
judgment is only regulative not constitutive. Though it

[1] Cf. *Lose Blätter*, i, pp. 19 f., and *Critique*, A. p. 181 = B. p. 223.
[2] And if it were not so, what places it beyond all question is Kant's idea
of an intuitive understanding different from our own with all the modal
distinctions that it entails. (Cf. *Kritik d. U.* § 77.)

has two ways of *considering* (*Beurtheilen*) material things,
it has no means of *determining* how they are actually
constituted. "In the unknown inner ground of nature
itself the mechanical and the teleological may be connected
in one *principle*: our reason, however, is not in a position
to unite them[1]."

Psychologically groundless as this assumption of a
reflective judgment as a faculty intermediate between
understanding and reason certainly seems to be, it had
nevertheless one important consequence for Kant. It led
him to excogitate a *Critique* dealing at last with the world
as a whole and with man as a whole. But then, as this
Critique moves on, the bounds of the supposed subordinate
faculty of judgment—which by the way Kant began by
identifying with common sense—steadily extend till in
the end it becomes a sort of intellectual rumination indistinguishable from reason[2]. In his first *Critique* Kant had
worked out an epistemological basis for a science of nature
embodying the principles formulated in his three analogies
of experience. This was all the science of nature that could
be called exact and constitutive. But he now found himself
confronted by facts which could not by any possibility be
made to fit into that mechanical scheme. Such were the
facts which a critical study of feeling and its implications
had meanwhile disclosed to him, facts which bridged a
gap in his philosophy that he had hitherto failed to
recognise. He now saw that to reconcile Nature (*i.e.* as
he had so far conceived it) with Freedom, teleology was
essential. The result, as we have seen was, first, to place

---

[1] *Op. cit.* § 70, p. 400.
[2] Cf. v. Hartmann, *Kant's Erkenntnistheorie und Metaphysik*, 1894,
pp. 234 f.

mechanism and teleology on a par: the relation of means and end must have a place along with that of cause and effect. In other words both proved to be categories involved in the 'possibility of experience'—his table of categories notwithstanding. Next, teleology was declared to be pre-eminent, inasmuch as it is essential if the world for us is to have any meaning at all. And lastly, the imperative behests of our own moral nature to promote the chief end of man made it reasonable to postulate a Supreme Author of Nature in order to insure for that end its final and complete realisation. Though no absolute proof (κατ' ἀλήθειαν) of the existence of such a being is theoretically forthcoming, yet for us (κατ' ἄνθρωπον) this postulate of reason, which is primarily practical, is all-sufficient[1]. So then, here as everywhere, our interpretation (*Beurtheilung*) of the world is anthropomorphic and reflective.

Anthropomorphism is Kant's own term: but unfortunately it is a term apt to suggest myths and graven images, fictions which at the best only travesty or mask the real truth. To condemn any and every use of it on this ground has seemed to many to be sound criticism: yet it is utterly shallow, as a little reflexion may shew. We have only to look back on the history of thought since intersubjective intercourse began, to see that it was the recognition of analogous relations between things differing in other respects, that first opened up the way to intelligent knowledge. The discernment of new differences alone would only have added to the confusion in which nothing was assimilated. Doubtless in the infancy of mankind, the *juventus mundi*—beyond the recognition of their fellow creatures—the anthropomorphisms in vogue were childish

[1] *Op. cit.* § 90, p. 477.

enough, as comparative mythology abundantly shews. Equally certain is it that steadily, as self-knowledge increased, we put away such childish things. But even when in this way we pass from what Kant called our 'intellectual minority' (*Unmündigkeit*) to the full 'age of reason' the anthropomorphic vein is still traceable, little as we are ordinarily aware of it. It is now, however, apparent not in sensible analogies (as when, for example, we recognise other living beings) but only in such analogies as Kant called symbolic. *À propos* of this he remarks: "Here is a business (*Geschäft*) which has not as yet been adequately set in order"; nevertheless he contents himself by referring to Locke[1]. Yet Locke, though professing to follow a 'plain historical method,' failed to reach the supreme principle of all 'understanding' whatever. This defect is specially striking in his strenuous but ineffectual efforts to obtain 'a clear and distinct idea' of what is meant by substance. In the end he was driven to aver that in using that term we still 'talk like children' and remind him of the poor Indian philosopher whom he has immortalized. Kant did far better: he clearly formulated the 'supreme principle of all use of the understanding[2]' which English empiricists with the exception of Berkeley failed to see. And yet he too failed, failed at least to realise all that this principle, the functional unity of self-consciousness in knowing, really meant.

Anthropomorphism, however, is not the best term to bring out the significance for knowledge of this central principle. A far preferable term would have been reflexion. But reflexion, duly defined for the purpose, of course;

---

[1] *Op. cit.* § 59, p. 364. Cf. Locke, *Essay*, III. i. 5.
[2] B. § 17.

since, when psychologically used by Locke and Hume, though not by Kant himself, as equivalent, that is to say, to what is now often called introspection, it only contributes to the material to be dealt with. Kant used the term 'transcendental reflexion' and this might have sufficed, had not his doctrine of the two stems of knowledge led him to misapply it. The reflexion here meant—epistemological reflexion we might now call it—belongs to a higher plane than that of the abstraction in which we turn away from the objective factor in experience while investigating the subjective. Here, with all the knowledge we have of both sides, we ponder and review the evolution of the whole. And such is very much what the reflective judgment in the end has turned out to be. It is reflexion that leads us theoretically to the idea of an understanding not our own but conformable to ours so far as the limits of our finite being allow. It is reflexion that leads us to subordinate mechanism to teleology, so long as we fail to transcend their seeming opposition. It is reflexion that suggests the Idea of the world as a realm of ends. Finally, it is reflexion that leads us in the practical sphere to postulate a Moral Ruler of this realm[1]. *Intelligendo se, intelligit omnia alia* has been said of God. It is the same truth, relatively valid for us, which underlies all the anthropomorphisms to be found in Kant's *Critiques*, whether avowed or not. Yet he failed to connect these branches with the single stem he had himself emphasized as the supreme principle. This failure we have already traced to his defective psychology, his misinterpretation of Newton, and his adherence to a formalism more extreme even than that of his old master, Wolff. But as Hartmann

[1] Such reflexion is what Dilthey has called *Selbstbesinnung*.

has aptly said: Like Moses he guided others to the promised land in which he believed but which he never reached himself[1].

Yet after all it was no promised land to which Kant pointed, but the merest mirage, unless one central tenet of his psychology—to which allusion has already been made[2]—proves to be invalid. I refer, I need hardly say, to his doctrine of *inner sense*. It behoves us then, as every Kantian commentator recognises, patiently and carefully to consider this doctrine, perplexing and tedious though the task may be.

§ 21. *The Doctrine of Inner Sense: (a) in the Æsthetic*

Kant's contemporaries for the most part had no special difficulty in conceding his doctrine concerning external sense, *viz.* that we cognise the world which confronts us, the Not-self, only so far as it appears to us through our senses. They had the less difficulty, because it was assumed that even if the data of external sense were merely appearances, at least they involved the reality of the self to whom they appeared. Kant, however, made no such reservation. He maintained, it will be remembered[3], that through sense-data we obtain no knowledge of anything beyond appearances, *i.e.* beyond the phenomenal world. The concept of a noumenal world, a world of so-called things *per se*, is for us, he maintained, entirely negative and problematic: it merely indicates an unattainable limit within which alone our positive experience lies. Accordingly he called his philosophy 'transcendental idealism.'

---

[1] Cf. von Hartmann, *op. cit.* p. 236.   [2] Cf. above, p. 92.
[3] Cf. above, pp. 33, 40.

But when by parity of reasoning he proceeded—as the doctrine of internal sense required—to maintain that our knowledge of the Self, like that of the Not-self, is confined to appearances, beyond which we have no knowledge of it at all—no wonder that cries of dissent and calls for explanation arose on every hand. "If the real existence of the subject is just as problematic as that of the object, if experience is nothing but appearances regressing *ad indefinitum*, is it not all an inexplicable illusion[1]? Moreover how could we even talk of appearances if we ourselves have no reality?" To this general clamour Kant in the second edition of his *Critique* was forced to reply; and many were the changes which he made in every part of it in consequence. He still, however, adhered to his assumption of an inner sense, thereby rendering the reality of the Self—which he had hitherto taken for granted—a problem which, now that it was raised, he could not satisfactorily solve. Before attempting to deal with this problem it will be well first to discuss the doctrine of the inner sense, on which it turns, apart.

We may begin by noting that Kant accepted a psychophysical generalisation which has prevailed since the days of Democritus at least. According to this, every sensation involves (1) a sense-organ which is extraneously 'stimulated,' as we now say; and (2) an awareness of a concomi-

---

[1] One striking passage bearing this out occurs in the course of certain observations Kant incidentally makes *à propos* of our sensibility. "The mystery of its origin, of its reference to (*Beziehung auf*) an object and what the transcendental ground of that unity [may be, all this]," he says, "lies without doubt far too deeply hidden for us—who know even ourselves only through inner sense—to be able to use an organon (*Werkzeug*) so unsuitable to discover anything besides again and again phenomena, whose non-sentient cause we yet would like to investigate." A. p. 278 = B. p. 334.

tant sense-datum on the part of the subject to which the organism pertained. In external sensation the something affecting is distinct from the subject affected, whereas in internal sensation the something affecting is the subject itself: otherwise the two cases are alike. This was Kant's initial position. But what does the subject affect? A sense-organ we naturally expect to be told. Not so, however: according to Kant the subject affects itself. The two cases then are not alike. How this self-affection is possible Kant admits to be a difficulty; but he consoles himself by saying that it is a difficulty common to all theories alike[1]. Surely this is not a reason for consolation, but a call for further inquiry. What about a sense-organ? for this question seems still to press. In the case of an external sense everybody comes to know what the organ concerned is; and Kant himself—*à propos* of 'the organ of the soul'—indulged on one occasion in some terribly crude speculations as to the mode in which the several external senses communicate with the soul[2].

But even in regard to an internal sense-organ, despite his statement that here the subject affects itself, Kant after all found something more to say. He then, however, goes to the opposite extreme: instead of finding the inner sense which is the organ of the soul, he thinks that "one might say that the soul [itself] is the organ of the inner sense[3]." It seems at first sight hopeless to attempt to make anything out of this, the more hopeless because Kant definitely rejected, as we shall presently see, any theoretical assumptions concerning a soul at all. How came he, then,

---

[1] B. p. 68.
[2] *Zu Sömmerring, über das Organ der Seele*, 1796, *Werke*, VI. pp. 459 ff.
[3] *Anthropologie*, *Werke*, VII. § 22, p. 474.

to refer to 'the soul' here? I will leave him to speak for
himself: "Because," he says, "there are not different
organs through which man is internally sensible of himself (*sich innerlich empfindet*), there is only one inner sense,
and so one might say the soul [in other words, the subject]
is the organ of inner sense." In short, Kant seems here to
be back at his main position that the subject affects itself.

Notwithstanding the stress just laid on the oneness of
the inner sense, we find him also talking of a special, an
interior, sense for pleasure-pain, distinct from the internal
sense, and in sundry places in the original text the plural
'inner senses' occur[1]. Moreover his whole treatment of
faculties implies that if it be allowable to recognise any
inner sense at all, there must needs be several. Surely
all this is a bad beginning: Kant's difficulty is where
it was.

But let us now look closer. It is generally held that our
several external senses have been gradually differentiated
from a primordial sense or coenaesthesis (Kant's *sensus
vagus*[2]), and what little Kant has said about these senses
is in keeping with this view. Each of the five senses now

----

[1] *Op. cit.* § 13. In the oral lectures on Metaphysics, delivered while he
was still at work on the *Critique*, Kant described rational psychology as 'the
knowledge of the object of *the inmost sense* (*innersten Sinne*).' Italics mine.
(Cf. B. Erdmann, article "Kant's metaphysical standpoint about 1774,"
Philos. Monatshefte, xx. (1884), p. 72 *fin.*) As to the plural usage cf. A.
p. 38=B. p. 55: "our inner senses (of myself and of my state)"; A. p. 381,
where '*Seelenlehre*' (psychology) as 'the physiology of the inner senses' is
compared with *Körperlehre* (physics) as the physiology of the objects of
the outer senses. A few editors regard the former as merely a clerical
error; and more so regard the latter, regardless of the presumption in
favour of the more difficult reading, against which there is no objection
on the score of being meaningless. In *Reflexionen*, II. 324, p. 101, *i.e.* in
Kant's *own* MS., 'inner senses' occurs twice.

[2] Cf. *Anthropologie*, § 14.

has a specific quality and at the outset one never has any connexion with another; though, through temporal and spatial relations, they eventually become complicated in the intuition of what we call physical Objects. Is there any parallel to all this in the development of self-consciousness? As strictly spatial relations are not here immediately involved, we have only to inquire (1) whether there is any evidence of a primitive internal sensation 'passively' received which is gradually differentiated into qualitatively distinct internal sensations; and (2) whether these become temporally complicated into the intuition of what we call the Self or the Subject.

As to the first question—Kant at all events produces no evidence of any connexion between the one inner sense and the special inner senses of which he also spoke. So far from being differentiated from one inner sense, the latter have nothing in common with sense at all. Moreover they actually precede it—the one inner sense—as it is described by Kant. For according to him, this inner sense, like the external senses, is concerned only with cognition. Hence the parallel between them from which he starts. The main difference is that the first have an objective reference, whereas the reference of the second is to the subject as 'affected by the play of its own thoughts' (or presentations, as I think we may say)[1]. The special inner senses, on the other hand, are concerned with feeling and conation, which as Kant repeatedly affirms are not cognitive

---

[1] *Anthropologie*, § 22 *init.* In a much earlier work dated 1762, Kant defines the inner sense as 'the faculty of making one's presentations into the object of one's own thoughts' (*Werke*, II. p. 68). This brings his inner sense closely into line with Locke's reflexion, of which, however, Locke had said—a point too often forgotten—"*though it be not sense...*yet it is very like it," a most unjustifiable and disastrous addition.

at all[1]. Yet both are more fundamental than the reflexion about 'the play of our presentations' which Kant's one inner sense implies. There is then in the case of this supposed inner sensibility no evidence of differentiation from a common basis such as the development of the external senses affords. What we come upon here, however, is just the three-fold nature, the three cardinal features, of all mental life, cognition, feeling and conation. But here the cognition is that of a higher level of experience than the level at which experience begins—in other words the cognition here is *not* sensory. That it is not, is shewn by Kant's reference to 'the play of our thoughts' and further by the remark that "the presentations of [the] external senses constitute the actual (*eigentlichen*) stuff" of inner intuition[2]. But since, as we have said, every sense is distinct from every other, it is obvious that internal intuition cannot be a special sense.

This remark of Kant's brings us to our second question, *viz.* whether all or any of the stuff with which, as he says, 'we beset our mind' (*unser Gemüth besetzen*)[3] becomes temporally complicated into the intuition of the subject, as the stuff of the external senses comes to be spatially complicated into the intuition of an outer object. We come here upon a new aspect of the parallel Kant is attempting to draw. As he began with two sorts of sense so he continues with two forms of intuition, which, *directly regarded*, are, like the senses, distinct from each

---

[1] Cf. *e.g.* B. p. 66.

[2] Cf. B. p. 67 and p. 50 *fin.*; also B. p. 37.

[3] A phrase, by the way, incompatible with pure passivity, and one moreover which Kant—in the very act of establishing this passivity—repeatedly uses; and the one, we may add, from which Fichte set out to refute him.

other. They are the spatial form in which the stuff of the
external senses is ordered, and the temporal form in which
the stuff of the internal sense is said to be ordered. The
two forms as such are distinct, since they have no characteristic in common. Different times are not together
whereas different spaces are; time is not determined by
space nor space by time; and a period of time has no
shape, while a portion of space has. But it seems impossible
to conceive experience as consisting of two parallel
sensory orders, one internal, the other external. Whatever
necessity there may be for the exposition of space and
time apart, yet there is no justification for ignoring their
invariable conjunction and mutual implication in fact.
But that is not all. It seems impossible even to give any
meaning to this coordination of internal and external,
unless something beyond them is implied, which is
distinct from either and related, from the very outset of
experience, to both. What is this something? Surely *the
subject itself*, which is not merely aware of the whole but
also interested in the whole, which not merely *cognises* it,
but at the same time *feels* in consequence of its presence,
and assumes a *conative* attitude towards it. And surely all
this must mean *some* subjective activity from the first.

Yet Kant's doctrine of an inner sensibility, here maintained, is incompatible with this. Between a pure activity—
his so-called 'intellectual intuition'—which is creative,
and a pure passivity—like that of wax to the impress of
a seal—which he called 'sensible intuition,' he allowed
no mean term. Then, however, 'sensible intuition' is a
flagrant misnomer, since intuition implies order and bare
sensations imply none. Out of sensations by themselves,
if such language has any meaning, no order can emerge.

This Kant fully allowed: he has himself said: "*that*, in which alone sensations are ordered and can be arranged in a certain form, cannot in turn be itself sensation; therefore, though the matter of appearances is given only *a posteriori*, their form must lie entirely ready, *a priori* in the mind (*im Gemüthe*), and hence can be considered separated from all sensation[1]." It is happily unnecessary to enter into the long and heated controversies which have been waged round this passage and its context[2]: at least the one point that concerns us now is clear. Kant allowed, as we too contend, that out of sensations as mere stuff, order and form can never arise: something ordering and informing is then implied, and surely this something cannot be devoid of all spontaneity.

At all events, it may be urged, the two cases, that of internal intuition and that of external intuition, were so far—for Kant himself at least—on a par; since the forms of both were said to lie ready in the mind (*das Gemüt*). But in the first place—Kant's psychological '*apriority*' apart[3] —his two so-called forms are not in fact on a par: very far from it. The perception of time is less sensuous, so to say, than that of space and is acquired later[4]. We find accordingly that the lower animals and children are soon quite

---

[1] A. p. 20 = B. p. 34. But forms lying ready to receive stuff, 'considered separately,' may suggest empty moulds: they certainly do not suggest a single informing activity.

[2] Cf. Vaihinger's *Commentar*, ii. (1892), pp. 56–88.

[3] In the *Æsthetic* it is abundantly evident that Kant began by using *a priori* in a chronological rather than in an epistemological sense. Cf. Vaihinger's excursus: 'How is Kant's *A priori* related to the Innate?' *Commentar*, ii. pp. 89–101.

[4] So, Kant thought there might be many forms of spatial intuition, but he did not contemplate any such possibility in the case of time. Cf. above, p. 88.

at home in space while children for long and the lower animals always, lack any clear ideas of time[1]. When Kant defined time as having but one dimension, *viz.* succession, he forgot that—though like all sentients we have always a succession of presentations—we only attain to a presentation of succession when we are conscious of our own duration and of the 'acts of attention' in which it is implied. Such acts he afterwards refers to in the *Analytic*[2], but here in the *Aesthetic*, they are altogether ignored. In the second place, even according to Kant's own exposition, these forms are not on a par, as we have already learnt from his references to 'the play of our thoughts' and to external intuition as the stuff with which internal intuition deals. These imply acts of attention: they may also involve feeling, but are not immediate affections of a sense.

It appears then that Kant's two kinds of sensibility, the internal and the external, are not comparable and do not run on all fours. This indeed is why the storm arose that he is now seeking to allay. The difference is that the subject is said to affect itself, though it knows itself *per se* as little as it knows the thing *per se* which also affects it. The difficulty is to make this intelligible. So far may we not say that he has not removed this difficulty? Though perhaps he has done something to alleviate it by using the vague and amphibious term, *Gemüt*. In the revised *Aesthetic*, for example, there is a somewhat bewildering alternation between the rôles assigned to the subject and its mind or *Gemüt*. Sometimes they seem to be identical: at others they are certainly distinct; and then at one time

---

[1] It was Kant's belief that animals have no inner sense at all. Cf. v. Hartmann, *Kants Erkenntnistheorie*, p. 52.

[2] B. p. 156 *n*.

the subject itself is active and affects the *Gemüt*, at another the *Gemüt* is active and affects itself. Finally, the subject is replaced by the faculty, elsewhere described as the capacity (*Fähigkeit*), of *becoming* self-conscious[1]. "If," Kant then states, "this faculty is to seek out (apprehend) what lies in the mind (*Gemüt*) it must affect that, and only in this manner can it bring forth, an intuition of itself." This intuition, however, will be merely sensible, for it is only apprehended in the mind, not immediately and spontaneously (*unmittelbar selbstthätig*) posited by the subject. It is, therefore, nothing more than the appearance of the subject *to* itself, as internally affected, not the subject as it is *in* itself[2].

Now what does all this seem to imply? Simply that a subject *capable* of self-consciousness, but not as yet self-conscious, has already a *Gemüt* (or mind) containing a 'manifold' ordered (*geordnet*) in the form of time. Whatever such subject may become, it has not, so far, got beyond the stage of apprehending: it does not comprehend, is only sentient, not intelligent. But sensibility Kant seems to connect specifically with the *Gemüt*. He speaks of that in this very same paragraph as 'through its own activity (*eigene Thätigkeit*) giving form to its sensory contents and thereby affecting itself[3].' This reminds us of Leibniz, who distinguished between an *automate spirituel* and the rational soul which is self-conscious[4]. *Gemüt*, as here used

[1] Much as psychologists in the present day talk of consciousness though they mean the experient subject itself.

[2] Cf. B. § 8, ii. pp. 67 ff.

[3] From much that Kant has said, it might be inferred—as indeed it has frequently been—that this activity is pre-conscious.

[4] Kant himself in the *Critique of the Practical Reason* likens Leibniz's *automate spirituel* to a machine worked by presentations. *Werke*, v. p. 101 *fin.*

by Kant, bears some resemblance to this *automate* of Leibniz, and still more perhaps to the 'psychical mechanism' we nowadays allow ourselves to talk of as that which we 'manipulate' in intellection[1]. It would not be very difficult on these lines to approximate Kant's process of seeking and bringing from the *Gemüt* an 'intuition of self' with the exposition nowadays frequently advanced as to the development of 'internal perception' or self-consciousness. It would, however, involve the abandonment of the doctrine of an 'inner *sense*,' root and branch; and for that Kant was not prepared. It would also involve the recognition of a certain continuity between the subjective activities which Kant in his revision of the *Aesthetic* alternately identified and distinguished. This brings us to his treatment of inner sense in the *Analytic*, where we shall find him making some advance, an advance which renders—if possible—the assumption of an inner sense still less tenable.

§ 22. *The Doctrine of Inner Sense: (b) in the Analytic*

In what this advance consisted we have already seen[2]: it consisted, it is hardly necessary to repeat, in the formulation of the unity of apperception as the transcendental condition (*i.e.* as the *sine qua non*) of all experience. For synthesis, the one constructive factor in experience, the presentation of which—as Kant maintained—'could never have been given through objects,' was to be traced entirely to 'the subject itself,' was, in fact 'an act of its own

---

[1] This would also obviate the suspicion that to deny an inner cause is necessarily to deny any difference between apperception and perception, as some have done. Cf. the writer's *Psychological Principles*, pp. 16, 372.

[2] Cf. above, pp. 49 f., 80 f.

spontaneity (*seiner Selbstthätigkeit*),' and so 'could not
be regarded as *belonging to its sensibility*[1].' *Prior* to such
active synthesis we cannot even talk of a determinate
object of cognition at all. According to the *Analytic* in
short, we find that the subject as cognitive is *never* purely
passive. This central truth, which Kant first propounded
and then obscured by his defective psychology[2], we for
our part have here to keep steadily before us[3].

We may begin by noting three points. *First*, though
occasional references to *das Gemüt* still recur, this is no
longer credited with a special activity, or spoken of as a
faculty. Like its equivalent English word 'mind' or the
Latin *animus*, it is used—as Kant elsewhere has expressly
said—to avoid the metaphysical implications of 'soul'
(*anima*)[4]. In short, *das Gemüt* is merely a general and
popular term denoting the experient subject together with
the presentations or objects of its experience; that whole
which it is the business of psychology to analyze. The
issue raised in the *Analytic* is, then, so far simplified.
Fundamentally we have to deal solely with the activity of
the experient subject itself. *Secondly*, we notice the dis-
appearance of the crude metaphor of ready-made forms,

[1] B. § 15, p. 130; § 15, p. 132. Italics mine.
[2] Cf. above, pp. 80 f. and 84 f.
[3] Into the various grades of synthesis which Kant distinguished in his
first edition as 'transcendental but yet unconscious' we scarcely need to
enter, since they were practically abandoned in the second, leaving only an
atrophied survival in the so-called 'productive imagination' mediating
between sense and understanding. But this again we may disregard as
merely an assumption consequent on Kant's original divorce of sensibility
from intellection. "These two," he afterwards said, "must be brought
together"; and yet in bringing them together, he ended by relegating
imagination to understanding. Cf. Volkelt, "*Kant's Stellung zum unbewusst
Logischen*," *Philos. Monatshefte*, IX. (1874), pp. 49 ff., 113 ff.
[4] Cf. *Zu Sömmerring, u.s.w., Werke*, VI. p. 458 *n*.

which sufficed for the treatment of space and time
according to Kant's original idea of sensibility as devoid
of spontaneity and merely passive. Now, we are expressly
told that the perception of space and time involves
synthesis; and the omission of any mention of this fact in
the *Aesthetic* is excused on expository grounds[1]. *Thirdly*,
we now learn that even the bare 'reception' of sense-data
or 'the manifold' that is synthesized, involves the activity
which all cognition implies. For a sense-datum is only
mine in so far as I am actually aware of it; a truth which
we express by saying "I think it," *i.e.* am conscious of it[2].

We have next to ask: with what is this subjective
activity as cognitive, directly concerned? According to
Kant himself, it is concerned directly with its objective
counterpart[3]. This objective counterpart is at first undetermined (*unbestimmt*) though determinable (*bestimmbar*);
and the whole business of the subject as cognitive is to
determine it; the subject being so far the determinant
(*das Bestimmende*)[4]. In connexion with such objective

---

[1] B. § 26, p. 160 *n.*, adumbrated in A. pp. 98 f. ('Of the Synthesis of
Apprehension'). *À propos* of Kant's method of exposition, Caird gives an
interesting quotation from Jachmann's biography, on which Caird himself
indulges later in some racy comments, *The Critical Philosophy of Kant*,
1889, I. pp. 64 and 283.

[2] Cf. B. § 16 *init.* and p. 134. This awareness or *Setzung*, enounced at
our level in an existential proposition, we have already found Kant recognising in the *Æsthetic* without taking account of its active implication (cf.
again B. p. 160 *n.*). Yet surely nothing could be more obvious than that
a judgment, whether it be 'I think' or 'It exists' cannot be a sensation.

[3] Herein we have the irreducible minimum of any experience at all—
the duality of subject and object.

[4] How Kant could allow himself to talk of the Ego or Self as ever
itself remaining merely *das Bestimmbare*, because it lacks a further intuition
of what *das Bestimmende* in itself may be, of which it is only conscious as
spontaneity—this is a question that has led more than one of his com-

determination Kant formulated what he called 'the principle of the synthesis of all possible predicates which are to make up the complete concept of a thing.' This organization of its knowledge of *objects*, we may therefore say, is the *sole* function of the subject as cognitive[1].

In all cognition, then, even in the initial awareness or appropriation of sense-data, the subject, as we have seen, is interested and active. This activity at the self-conscious level finds expression in an existential proposition, recognised by Kant himself as a *Setzung* or 'positing[2].' But if the subject is active even in acknowledging what, willy nilly, is there confronting it, can it be said to be merely passive when what confronts it are those acts whereby it organizes its knowledge, acts which at the self-conscious level it reflectively refers to itself, and recognises as its own? The whole teaching of Kant's *Analytic* as to this question is emphatically in the negative. Cognition,

mentators to exclaim. Cf. B. p. 158 *n*. and p. 407, and Benno Erdmann's *Kant's Kriticismus* (1878), p. 215.

[1] A. p. 572 = B. p. 600. This we may regard as a regulative principle directive of the constitutive principles of synthesis. It implies the pragmatic law (or maxim) of subjective selection, *viz.* that objective differentiation proceeds on subjectively determined lines, in other words that knowledge is pursued for the sake of self-conservation or self-realisation: cognitive activity, that is to say, is essentially practical. Cf. the writer's *Psychological Principles*, p. 414.

[2] "Is the subject not affected as well as active?" some Kantian may rejoin. Unquestionably the subject is incidentally affected; for it is never merely cognitive. In any situation of which it is definitely aware, it is, in general, either pleased or pained. Such purely subjective states are, however, always to be distinguished from whatever cognitions may be their immediate occasion; for such cognitions are objective, directly involving activity, not affectivity. On this difference, Kant himself, as we have already seen, insisted (cf. above, p. 57). When then he allows himself to attribute feeling to an 'interior sense' we can only dismiss this as but one instance of his frequent inconsistency in respect to terminology.

according to that, is never, even when non-voluntary,
entirely passive, least of all then in that self-consciousness,
the unity of which is the ground and source of all the
categories, the original unity of apperception. Moreover,
Kant insists on distinguishing this from the inner sense,
with which he thinks psychologists have generally confused it[1]. Having gone so far, it seems strange that Kant
did not go further; for careful and cautious analysis of
self-consciousness was certainly the crying need of
psychology at that time. But instead of attempting to
solve this problem, Kant simply prejudged it, as Herbart
has well said[2], by assuming 'as its foundation-stone' the
current doctrine of an inner sense, which he never made
the faintest attempt to examine or discuss. Nevertheless
it is a doctrine that the whole trend of his *Analytic*, as
already said, altogether discredits.

And yet with almost blind perversity Kant professed to
find in the *Analytic* the proper place to explain this paradox
—as he calls it—of the inner sense, which in the *Aesthetic*
had been left as 'a difficulty common to all theories alike[3].'
But he only repeats the incongruities we have noticed
above; save that he now, as already said[4], makes some
advance by transferring the rôle of the *Gemüt* as active to
the understanding. This, he says, "exerts that action on
the *passive subject, whose faculty it is,* which entitles us to
say that thereby the inner sense is affected[5]." This process
he calls 'figural synthesis,' since all the understanding

---

[1] B. p. 153. The truth being rather that they did not understand inner
sense as literally as Kant himself did.

[2] *Psychologie*, 1850, § 125, II. p. 189.

[3] B. § 24, pp. 152–4. Cf. B. § 8, p. 58.

[4] Cf. above.

[5] *Loc. cit.* p. 153. Italics mine.

does so far is to influence the imagination, which is always
sensuous. In that case, if the inner sense were coeval with
the outer senses, we should expect the lower animals to
be self-conscious; but Kant had maintained that they
have no inner sense. Then, however, it would be reasonable to suppose that for what he called 'intellectual (*i.e.*
categorial) synthesis,' in distinction from the merely
'figural' synthesis of imagination, self-consciousness was
essential—and in fact the two are always found together.
Considerations of this sort then, we repeat, ought, one
would think, to have led Kant to undertake a systematic
inquiry into the genesis of self-consciousness, instead of
being content to work—so to say by rule of thumb—
with the crude faculty psychology he found ready to his
hand[1].

But notwithstanding his professed preference for epigenesis in place of preformation[2], his whole treatment of
the present topic seems to be entirely on the lines of the
latter. He talks as if the whole formal apparatus of
experience were complete potentially before experience
began—categorial equally with figural synthesis[3]. However perplexing and vexatious as his commentators for
the most part have found even Kant's attempts in the
second edition to dissipate the objections raised against
his doctrine of inner sense in the first—he himself was so
satisfied with the result, that he ends by now exclaiming

[1] Much as he had been content to begin his search for a system of
categories from the table of judgments, which, as he professed, 'the work
of the logicians provided ready to his hand.' Cf. above, p. 44.

[2] Cf. B. § 27, p. 167 and above, p. 55.

[3] Thus he remarks: "Apperception with its synthetic unity...under the
designation of categories relates to (*geht auf*) objects as such prior to all
sensuous intuition." B. § 24, p. 154.

that he does not see why so much difficulty is found in admitting it[1]. Yet, some four years later still, he again admitted 'nothing to be stranger or more surprising' than this very doctrine. That the Ego can be known (*bekannt*) to itself only as a phenomenon of the inner sense, *i.e.* as an object in time, not as thing *per se*, which as subject it is, this he now declares to be an 'undoubted fact, but one which it is utterly impossible to explain[2].' Well, it is an undoubted fact that when at length we have attained to self-consciousness we can distinguish between our knowledge of self—the so-called 'empirical Ego'—and the subject that we must be to have this knowledge—the so-called 'pure Ego.' But it is further an undoubted fact that this knowledge—gradually built up by intersubjective intercourse—has turned out to be utterly inexplicable when traced back to a sense. For is it not now clear—as the distinguished psychologist W. Volkmann has said[3]— that "the entire fiction of an inner sense is nothing but an attempt to solve a problem which can never find its solution in the sphere of sense"? Finally, is it not obvious that a statement involving incompatible positions must in fact be false? If the subject were only known 'like other objects'—Kant's own words more than once repeated[4]— *i.e.* as phenomenal, what warrant should we have for affirming that it exists as thing *per se*? If we are entitled to assert this existence, must not that differentiate it altogether from objects, the existence of which as its object presupposes its own existence?

[1] B. § 24, p. 156 *n*.
[2] *Ueber die Fortschritte der Metaphysik u.s.w.*, written for a Berlin Academy prize announced for 1791, *Werke*, VIII. p. 530.
[3] *Lehrbuch der Psychologie*, 2te Aufl. (1876), II. p. 182.
[4] Cf. B. p. 155, B. p. 429, and *Werke*, VIII. p. 531.

§ 23. *The Doctrine of Inner Sense: (c) in the Dialectic*

So we come at length to the second part of our inquiry[1]; for after all Kant's supposed inexplicable fact was really for him a serious problem. There is, however, no genuine problem here at all. The common sense belief in the actuality (*Wirklichkeit*) of the subject of experience together with the common sense belief in the actuality of the correlative object of experience, Kant did right in not questioning. The duality of subject and object in experience—no subject here without its object and no object here save for a subject, as Fichte strenuously maintained —this is our bedrock fact. There can, in short, be no appearances without an objective reality that appears and no appearing of that reality without a subjective reality to which it appears. The fatal defect of Kant's transcendental idealism consisted in sundering the appearances declared to be alone knowable from the actual realities which he never questioned, but declared nevertheless to be unknown and unknowable. This defect—the Achilles' heel of Kant's philosophy—is the source of his epistemological problem, which we must now attempt to unravel[2].

In this part of our inquiry we have mainly to deal with the first division of Kant's *Dialectic*, *viz.*, the so-called Paralogisms of Pure Reason, the self-sophistications, that is to say, whereby reason according to Kant's *Critique* has deluded itself into hypostasizing the mere *Idea* of a pure subject. Thus, by what is doubtless *par excellence* the metaphysician's fallacy—the concreting of abstractions— the rational psychology then in vogue maintained the existence of an unconditional unity, the simple substance

[1] See above, p. 140.   [2] Cf. above, pp. 61 and 76.

called soul as *ens per se subsistens*. Though he proceeds to
expose the fallacy, Kant, it is important to notice, adopted
the Idea. As 'regulative' it served as a *'focus imaginarius,'*
unifying and systematizing the manifold results of empirical psychology. But taken as 'constitutive,' *i.e.* as
itself corresponding to something concrete and actual, it
became an *ignis fatuus* luring reason to disaster. Kant's
own version of this Idea given in the final summary
appended to the *Dialectic* is instructive enough to justify
a brief digression. It is, he says, the Idea of one's self
regarded 'as merely thinking nature or soul'—a most
inadequate idea, of course. Reason here derives from 'the
empirical unity of all thinking' this Idea of 'an unconditioned and original unity,' *i.e.* a simple substance personally identical, which interacts with other actual things
outside it, in a word, the idea of a simple, self-existing
(*selbständig*) intelligence. This Idea, however, points not
to an 'ostensive concept,' but merely provides a heuristic
fiction, whereby the maximum of unity and system may
be imparted to our knowledge. It does not assume what
the actual ground of the attributes of the soul may be;
"for these can have quite other grounds, of which we
know nothing at all[1]."

An Idea, which as 'make believe,' an 'as if' (*als ob*), is
to prove a guiding star, but which, genuinely believed in
as really true, can only beguile and betray—this is surely
something new and strange in the history of thought.
What is opined in the first case, would, so far as it came
to be verified, accord with what in the other was affirmed

[1] This account given in the first edition (A. p. 682) is retained unaltered
in the second (B. p. 710) though inconsistent in many respects with the
changes made in that. Cf. *Methodology*, A. p. 771 = B. p. 799.

from the first. If, however, as Kant maintained, no empirical verification is ever possible, are we not living in a fool's paradise if we pretend to unify *knowledge* by a fiction concerning the unknowable? But it should now be observed that in Kant's version of the Idea the start is made from a *fact*, to wit 'the empirical unity of all thinkings'; also that here, as often elsewhere, he talks about the soul as freely as his opponents. Moreover, had he not, biassed by his fanciful and mischievous 'architectonic,' more or less travestied the rational psychology he is supposed to be controverting, he would not have failed to notice that it too started from the same fact[1].

But now returning to the Paralogisms—wherein Kant traces the fallacy of rational psychology through all the divisions of his table of categories—we have first of all to note that in his first edition Kant, here as elsewhere, proceeded entirely oblivious of the antithetic position which his doctrine of inner sense involved. So far from being conscious that the reality even of the self—to say nothing of the nature of a soul—was for him a *problem*, he seems nowhere to have been at the trouble to say—as he afterwards said—that at any rate it was for him 'an undoubted fact.' The changes he was led to make in his second edition[2] when at length the problem confronted

----

[1] Wolff, for example, certainly did not make the 'I think' the sole text of his rational psychology, nor separate this from empirical psychology as, according to Kant's doctrine of things *per se*, they must be separated. Cf. I. E. Erdmann's longer *Gesch. d. neuern Philos*. Bd. ii. Abt. ii (1842), § 22, pp. 314 ff. and the *Belegstellen*, pp. cxxx ff. In fact, the rational psychology that Kant was refuting was substantially his own; though he was influenced, no doubt, by Knutzen, Reimarus and Mendelssohn. Cf. J. B. Meyer's *Kants Psychologie* (1874), pp. 275 ff.

[2] Already adumbrated in the *Prolegomena* (cf. §§ 46–50) published (1783) between the two.

him, are what now chiefly interest us. Rational psychology is, as the Americans say, a living proposition no more: the main issue of Kant's dialectic concerning that we may, therefore, now leave aside[1].

There is, however, one mistake which Kant shared with his dogmatic opponents. Both alike begin by treating of the so-called pure or transcendental Self as if it were an object. *Ex vi termini*, there is no possible experience in which the Self or Subject can be so regarded. Any knowledge we may come to acquire about it is knowledge of it in relation to the 'Non-Ego' or Not-Self with which throughout experience it interacts. The 'inconvenience' over which Kant seems to make merry, *viz.*, that the subject would have to become its own object in order to know itself as subject, and so be condemned to revolve in a perpetual circle—like a dog trying to catch its own tail, as we might say—till it realises the fatuousness of its attempt: all this is wholly imaginary, if it be meant to have any bearing on the process of becoming self-conscious. No doubt in that reflexion on *experience*—whereby we gain our knowledge about the Self—we make *that* an object of thought, but the knowledge thus attained is none the less knowledge of the Self, the subject experiencing, not about any object of its experience, *i.e.* its Not-Self.

The most perplexing thing in Kant's *Dialectic* here is just this lack of fixed orientation, which he seemed to

---

[1] One remark, however, is worth making: to expose the fallacies of an argument settles nothing as to the ultimate question at issue. This obvious truth Kant forgot (cf. B.421 *init.*); perhaps the more readily as the rational psychology he was here refuting was, as already said, that which he had long maintained as the true one, and continued to uphold in his oral lectures even while excogitating this *Critique*. Cf. note 1 opposite; and p. 82 *n*. 1.

think inevitable. Thus, in common with too many psychologists, he is obsessed by the confusion of the subject that is conscious with the so-called 'contents' of its consciousness; as if its very being consisted in its relation to its objects. In both editions, for example, he identifies the self (*das denkende Wesen*) with 'the mere consciousness' or 'the mere form of the consciousness,' which accompanies (*begleitet*) all presentations, and converts them into knowledge[1]. Now in the *Refutation of Idealism*, an important amendment in his second edition, he reached the following conclusion: "The consciousness of my own existence is at the same time an immediate consciousness of the existence of other things besides myself[2]." What is this but the recognition of the duality of subject and object in consciousness, *i.e.* in experience? How then can the subject alone be called 'the mere form' of consciousness?

Again Kant bewilders both himself and his readers by the meaning which he often puts on the Cartesian 'I think[3].' He then takes *Cogito* as implying thought only in the narrower sense of intellection, and as therefore not implying existence. For it was Kant's merit in agreement with Hume to insist that existence is not a predicate and cannot be intellectually 'posited[4].' No mere thinking of an object will justify the assertion that it exists: this he repeats again and again. "Thinking, as such," he says, "is merely the logical function...of synthesizing the manifold of a *possible* intuition[5]." Now in the bare proposition, 'I think,' which according to him is 'the sole text of

---

[1] A. p. 346 = B. p. 404; and again A. p. 382. As to the phrase *begleitet*, cf. above, p. 54 *n.*
[2] B. p. 276.
[3] Cf. B. p. 406.
[4] Cf. p. 15 above.
[5] B. p. 428. Italics mine.

rational psychology,' all reference to *actual* intuition is necessarily excluded; for otherwise the psychology would lapse to the empirical level. 'I think' then is *here* a merely logical proposition, and its subject only an abstraction. Therefore, Kant argues, in such a proposition I am not presented 'either as I am or as I appear, but I only think myself like any other object regarded as possible'—*i.e.* 'problematically.' All we have is just the empty idea of a subject in general as an object, not a something actually posited but only a something thought of. So far it is immaterial whether we say 'I think' or 'he thinks' or 'it thinks,' save that the impersonal form is the most general and commits us least[1]. In any case we have only 'a pronoun [standing for] a thing of uncertain connotation, *viz.*, the [logical] subject of all predicates[2].' The predicates here are thoughts. To these this 'problematic' and undetermined X is supposed to be attached (*angehängt*), or again they are supposed to inhere in it as a substance, or even to be merely accidents pertaining to it, of which we can imagine it to be divested. But surely all such suppositions are no better than a tissue of incongruities.

Let us glance back at the two chief points, beginning with the last. The *subject of sundry propositions* may be said to be 'attached to its predicates' (by the copula); and these may be said to be its attributes, if the propositions are analytical, and to be its accidents if they are not. Thoughts, however, of whatever kind, may, as presentations, be called objects, but cannot be called predicates, of *the subject of experience*[3]. The predicates of this are what the

[1] Cf. B. p. 429, A. p. 346 = B. p. 404.

[2] *Metaphysische Anfangsgründe, Werke,* IV. p. 438.

[3] If they could, Kant could not have called this subject 'the poorest of all presentations.' B. p. 408.

Idea of the subject is said to yield as the constitutive essence of it, according to the dogmatic rationalists, and as a regulative principle about it, according to the critical rationalism of Kant himself.

As to the other point—no doubt 'I think' *can* be treated as simply a logical proposition—like Apollo darts or Circe charms—without implying that the subject is here less 'problematic' than the subjects there. But the 'I think' with which we have now to deal is that involved in the 'originally transcendental unity of apperception.' There, however, 'I think' is an existential, not a merely logical proposition, or predication. It states an act, that is to say, a fact. "Only inasmuch as I can conjoin a manifold of presentations in *one [moment of] consciousness* is it possible for me to conceive (*vorstellen*) the identity of the consciousness in these presentations themselves: in other words, the *analytic* unity of consciousness is only possible on presupposition of some sort of synthetic [*i.e. synthesizing*] unity." Such was Kant's explicit declaration in the Deduction of the Categories[1]. But here in the Paralogisms it is only with the analytic unity that he is concerned: the *original* synthesizing—from which, as he said, "many things follow[2]"—he seems meanwhile to have forgotten. Accordingly he blames the rationalists for going back to the fact of the synthesizing unity and contends for confining psychology to the analytic unity simply[3]. *All this is consequential on his treatment of the real subject of experience as an object and confusing this object with a logical subject[4].*

---

[1] § 16. B. p. 133. Italics Kant's   [2] *Loc. cit.* p. 133 *init.*
[3] Cf. B. pp. 416–418.
[4] The subject, in short, becomes a *res incompleta*, the object of an impossible abstraction from the primordial duality of experience; and as

When, however, Kant takes Descartes' *Cogito* as Descartes meant it to be taken, the whole situation is altered. "The proposition 'I think,'" he then says, "so far as it is equivalent to 'I exist thinking' is not merely a case of logical function; on the contrary, it determines the subject (*which then is also object*) existentially." "This determination," he continues, "cannot take place without the inner sense," and sense never presents (*an die Hand giebt*) an object as thing *per se*, but merely as appearance[1]. At this point Kant's problem clearly emerges, and he had the courage to preface his discussion of it almost in the words of one of his ablest critics. "It looks," he says, "as if, according to our theory, the soul entirely and altogether —even in thinking—were reduced (*verwandelt*) to a phenomenon, and [as if] in such wise our very consciousness must, in fact, as mere illusion lead to nothing (*auf nichts gehen*)[2]." All suspicion of such 'illusion,' Kant felt must at any cost be dispelled.

§ 24. *Kant's treatment of the resulting problem*

But this new problem was not at all concerned about the nature of a *soul* nor immediately about the implications of *consciousness*. The problem was to hold fast to the *reality* of the self without at the same time repudiating the doctrine of transcendental idealism, *i.e.* that the self is only 'given' by an inner sense and so as *phenomenal*. Kant

such, merely the logical subject of the only true proposition that can be stated about it, *ego sum cogitans*; it is then meaningless, like one term of a real relation sundered from the other.

[1] B. p. 429. I have italicised Kant's parenthesis by way of recalling the strictures made above. Cf. pp. 159 f.

[2] B. p. 428.

had quite rightly started by regarding the real existence
of self as the fundamental fact; but then his doctrine of an
inner sense cut the ground from under this ultimate
position. No refutation of fallacies supposed to be inherent
in 'the very nature of reason' could restore that. Formal
errors of reasoning can involve no illusions, for illusions
are never formal; and in questions of fact where there is
nothing, there can be no illusion. I cannot say I am
nothing, whatever may be meant when I say that I am.
The problem, in short, is *not* as to *what* this I may be, the
existence of which every self-conscious being affirms for
itself in saying: I am.

In discussing that affirmation, however, Kant, as we
have seen, in common with the rationalist whom he was
bent on refuting, regarded the subject of experience as
merely an object of thought. In the first edition of the
Critique—before the existence of this subject had emerged
as a problem for him—he argued on the assumption that
the nature of this subject-object or logical subject was to
be determined, as in the case of other objects, by applying
to it the pure categories[1]. *So far* transcendental subject
and transcendental object were on a par, and (being
unknown) were also so far indistinguishable: hence he
came to talk of both indifferently as objects[2], despite the
all-important fact that the unity of apperception pertains
to the subject alone. But in a final summing up concerning the 'transcendental illusion' of the paralogisms
he remarks: "Of the thinking ego or 'soul' one can say
that it does not *know itself through the categories*, but on

[1] "The attributes, which I predicate of myself as a thinking being in
general, are no more than pure categories...." A. p. 399. Cf. also p. 401.
[2] Cf. above, p. 85.

the contrary...knows the *categories* through itself." He
then continues: "now it is surely very obvious that I
cannot know as itself an object that which I must presuppose in order to know any object at all[1]." "Nevertheless," he goes on to say, "nothing is more natural...
than the illusion of taking the unity in the synthesis
of thoughts [*i.e.* the unity of the categories] as a unity
perceived in the subject of these thoughts." We first
hypostasize consciousness, and then surreptitiously iden-
tify it with the subject that is conscious. We have got
what will prove a regulative idea, and mistake it for a
concrete reality.

In the second edition this argument, used in the first
to refute false assumptions concerning the *nature* of the
self, seems to have suggested to Kant the happy thought
that at least it sufficed to evince the *reality* of the self.
The former negative argument is thus turned to positive
account. Where he ended there, here he now begins. But
instead of saying that the subject cannot be known as an
object of the categories, he now begins by saying that the
modes of self-consciousness in thinking as such are not
yet categories, and so the consciousness of the determining
(*bestimmende*) self cannot be an object[2]. Then coming
presently to the existential 'position I am' which the 'I
think' involves, the question arises what does this mean?
It was in endeavouring to answer that question that Kant
made his final effort to establish the reality of the self
without *overtly abandoning* a tenet of his system so integral
as that of 'inner sense.'

It will be well to quote at length the greater part
of Kant's concluding statements on this point: "My

[1] A. p. 402. Cf. above, p. 82.   [2] Cf. B. p. 407.

existence," he says, "cannot be regarded as deduced from
the proposition 'I think'...but is identical with it. It [the
existential position] expresses an indeterminate (*unbe-
stimmte*) empirical intuition, *i.e.* perception...but it *precedes* the experience which is to determine the object of
the perception through the category in respect to time;
and existence here is further not the category[1]....An indeterminate perception here signifies only *something Real*
that has been given, and [given] indeed just for thinking
at all; and so *not as phenomenon nor as thing (Sache) in itself
(noumenon) but only as something that in fact exists*, and
[that] is designated as being such (*als solches*) in the
proposition 'I think.' For it is to be noted that in calling
that proposition empirical, I do not intend to say the Ego
in it is an *empirical presentation*: it is, on the contrary,
purely intellectual, since it pertains to any thinking at all.
But yet without *some empirical presentation or other* to
furnish *matter* for thinking, the *act* (Actus) [expressed
by] 'I think' would not take place. The empirical however
is only the condition of the application or of the use of the
pure intellectual faculty[2]."

Here we have a number of intermingled statements
supposed to be consilient, and together to yield the solution
which Kant is seeking of the problem he had previously
overlooked. First we are told that something Real is
meant which is not phenomenal; but yet something that
in fact exists, and is so designated in the proposition 'I
think'; also that I, the subject of this proposition, is not
here an empirical presentation. On the other hand we

[1] As referring to an *object*, of which we have a concept and wish to
know whether it can be 'posited' or not.
[2] B. p. 422 *n*. Italics mine.

are told that this proposition expresses an indeterminate empirical perception; but this perception is one which precedes the experience in which a schematized category (implying existence in time) is used. Further we are told that the empirical is only the *condition*[1] of the act, expressed by 'I think,' which is *applied* to it, and is therefore presupposed by it, being, in fact, the act of a purely intellectual faculty, 'given' as already said, before experience. External sense as the occasion for the exercise of this faculty is doubtless implied; and Kant has said (in a parenthesis, for clearness omitted above), that the existential 'I think' involves sensibility (*Sinnlichkeit*). Of course, as we have had so often to recall, object is correlative to subject. 'Something or other' besides the Ego there must be if there is to be experience; but it will not be something 'given' by any inner sense. Inner sense, according to Kant's own account, can only yield a perception in the form of time, and cannot therefore be indeterminate; since both form and sense (matter) are implied; nor can it precede experience.

Finally we come to the statement that this real which is not a phenomenon is also not a noumenon. What this means is not at once clear, for Kant has distinguished a double use of noumenon. If by this term "we understand a thing *so far as it is not* [*an*] *object of our sentient intuition* ...then that is a noumenon *in the negative* sense; if however we understand by it *an object of a non-sentient*,...*i.e.* intellectual, intuition...this would be the noumenon in a positive sense[2]." We have here two faulty definitions each

---

[1] It would have been better if he had said 'a condition or the occasion.'

[2] B. p. 307.

involving a negative term[1]. Also the positive noumenon is a negative noumenon as well, so far as 'an object of non-sentient intuition' is 'not an object of our sentient intuition.' Either way the *connotation* of noumenon—the thing as thought—is not identical with that of thing *per se* —the thing as it is: more generally, being is distinct from any knowledge of it. But since knowledge implies being —though we cannot say that being implies knowledge— the concept of things *per se*, things as being, is involved in Kant's concept of noumenon. We must pause then for a moment to note the connexion. As to positive noumena—these, we learn, answer to created beings regarded from the standpoint of their Creator, whose *thoughts* are things, such things as we know only by their appearance to us[2]. Thus from the divine standpoint things *per se* are positive noumena, are Reals; from ours they are only negative noumena, *i.e. only* thoughts of what is not impossible, *entia rationis*[3]. Accordingly Kant disallows the division of objects into phenomena and noumena, unless the term noumena is understood in this negative sense. And then it is tantamount to a division into what is empirically known as '*given*' in sense, and what is beyond this and merely '*thought* as logically possible.' It is in keeping with this division that he asserts the Ego to be neither phenomenon nor noumenon but something Real that in fact exists, the Ego as intelligence and thinking Subject, as he had already said[4].

At length we can return to what is the gist of Kant's

[1] For non-sentient intuition Kant does indeed substitute intellectual intuition. But this concept, for which he often used intelligible intuition he allows to be for us unintelligible.

[2] Cf. B. § 8, iv. [3] Cf. A. p. 290 = B. p. 347.

[4] B. p. 155.

present problem. This Ego, which is not an empirical presentation but a *sine qua non* of all presentation and so said to be 'given' before any presentation is possible, what exactly does it stand for (*bezeichnen*)? It is not a thought, for if it were, or could be, in the first instance merely thought, it would be only problematic; and how then could experience begin? Yet this, as we have seen, was the cardinal point round which the dialectic of the paralogisms turned. But we are beyond that point now. The thinking subject as existing cannot presuppose the categories for they, so far as modes of consciousness, presuppose it[1]. Now categories, it is well to remember, were primarily predicaments or predicational functions. But it is a peculiarity of two of Kant's categories, *viz*., existence and substance that, as he has himself said, they are not predicates[2]. As to Existence—we have already found him maintaining in one of his earliest works that existence "is in no sense a predicate or determination of anything whatever"; that on the contrary, "it is the absolute positing of the thing, and thereby distinguished from any and every predicate[3]." Later on, however, Kant came to speak of existential propositions not as positional but as propositional; but even then existence was not a *real* predicate[4]. As to Substance—it is the pure category which in transcendental logic represents that function, the form of which

[1] Moreover they are only applicable to external objects. Cf. B. p. 291.

[2] "There are two concepts which are not properly predicates of things, but by reason of which the things themselves are thought along with all their predicates." *Reflexionen*, p. 566.

[3] Cf. above, pp. 14 ff. For this reason it had but a dubious standing in the table of categories and in the synthetic principles. Cf. Adickes, *Systematik*, pp. 35, 54, Norman Smith, *Commentary*, pp. 193 f. and 391 ff.

[4] Cf. the writer's article in *Mind*, xxviii. (1919), pp. 259 ff.

is expressed in a categorical proposition: in other words it relates to what is always thought to exist as subject and never as predicate[1]. As such it was placed by Aristotle before all other categories and regarded as the only one that could stand apart; in respect of which the remaining categories were only accidental and relative. It was, therefore, a defect of Kant's table of categories that these two were lined up with the rest, instead of their primary and distinctive character being indicated from the first. The Ego then as existing subject is neither predicated nor postulated but absolutely posited as the *sine qua non* of 'the radical faculty of all our knowledge.'

The only possible meaning of the statement that the Ego is neither phenomenon nor noumenon but something Real actually and actively existing, seems now clear: the Ego is in Aristotle's sense a substantial factor in experience not a mere attribute of it[2]. Here then, we may say again that Kant has advanced beyond his critical standpoint as based on transcendental idealism. According to that, we start from sense-data as subjective affections passively received. Having called these appearances[3] (*phenomena*), we are obliged, when it comes to thinking, to *think* them related to things behind or beyond them which never appear (*noumena*), in order to avoid the absurdity of an appearance without anything that appears[4]. So we advance to the *Notbegriff* of the negative noumenon, which is only

---

[1] Cf. B. § 14 *fin.*

[2] Cf. *Fortschritte der Metaphysik, Werke,* VIII, p. 531:—"The subject of apperception is comparable with the Substantial that remains when all the accidents inhering in it are *left out.*"

[3] When and how we come to do so, Kant neglected to inquire. Neither genetic nor transcendental psychology was in his line.

[4] Cf. A. p. 250, B. preface, p. xxvi.

problematic, not positional—to which, therefore, the categories, as valid only for phenomena, do not apply. Now Kant is constrained to admit that these categories which are applicable only to presented objects have their source in the intelligent subject which thus applies them. His exposure of the rational psychology of the Wolffians may be sound enough as regards the conclusions reached; but it was not sound in the contention from which it started[1], *viz.*, that the Idea of the Self is simply a *focus imaginarius*, which reason, unchecked by transcendental idealism, mistakes for a thing *per se*. And he only escaped from the conclusions of a sensationalist psychology like Hume's by unconsciously abandoning the doctrine of inner sense. So he continued to imagine that his system remained unchanged, since through all he had never doubted the reality of things *per se*. In this, however, as one of his ablest expositors has remarked, he only sophisticated himself[2]. The change is unmistakeable, though he did not see it. What he did not see was that 'inner sense' is a misnomer for something radically different.

As already said, the first indication of Kant's awakening to the problem which the critics of his transcendental idealism disclosed to him is to be found in the *Prolegomena*. In the second edition of the *Critique* he made no further reference to what he had there said. Still it is too interesting to be passed over altogether, so we may briefly notice it here. He began by recapitulating the main position of his

---

[1] Cf. Hegel's summary *à propos* of the Paralogisms:—"By his polemic against the old metaphysics......Kant did well; but when he came to state his reasons, his failure is apparent." *Encyclop.* I. § 47 *fin.* p. 101. So rendered by Wallace.

[2] Cf. Erdmann, *Kant's Kriticismus in der ersten und in der zweiten Auflage*, 1878, p. 223.

transcendental idealism, *viz.*, that the discursive nature of
our understanding debars us from ever attaining to an
actual knowledge of anything corresponding to the Idea
of a thing in itself—a subject that cannot be in turn a
predicate. He then supposes, as was maintained by his
critics, that we have in the conscious Self not merely an
Idea but the *absolute* Subject itself given in experience.
"This expectation," he proceeds to say, "proves to be
vain. For the Ego is no concept at all but merely [the]
designation of the object of the inner sense." And he adds
in a note—and this is the interesting point—"The presentation of apperception, the Ego...is nothing more than
[the] feeling of an existence (*eines Dasein*)...to which all
thinking stands in relation (*relatio accidentis*)."

Here, in the first place, the Ego of apperception is
generically defined as *feeling*. Obviously this could not be
said of the transcendental object. Despite Kant's transcendental idealism, subject and object are then not on a
par. Here, however, what he saw was that the Ego of
apperception is neither a definite intuition nor a concept
nor yet the mere form of consciousness[1]. But such
negatives do not suffice to sustain its reality. So the happy
thought occurs to him that it is feeling—a thought to
which he never returned, but a pregnant one, none the
less. Though feeling is never a complete state of consciousness, it is the most central one, as Kant came at long last
to recognise. Had he at this juncture been awake to the
considerations that dawned upon him in working out his
third *Critique*[2], his whole doctrine of the Self might well
have been different. But following, as he usually did, the
method prescribed by his architectonic conception of

[1] Cf. A. p. 382.   [2] Cf. above, p. 102.

system[1], in other words, confining himself within 'water-tight' compartments, he—with this single exception—treated the problem of the Self solely from the standpoint of thought[2].

In the second place, the feeling in which the Ego of apperception is said to consist, is further defined *specifically* as feeling of *a presented existence*; for such is the primary meaning of *Dasein*, 'being there.' A presented existence, however, is just an object among other objects[3]; and that is what the pure Ego of apperception is not, and cannot be; as Kant in his final discussion of the paralogisms came to see. It is this familiar antithesis of 'here' and 'there' that we use, more or less metaphorically, to represent the fundamental antithesis of subject and object; in terms, that is to say, of our ultimate schema of relations, *viz.* space.

But there is still one further remark to make. In this same passage Kant refers to 'appercipient Ego' as only a '*designation*' (*Bezeichnung*) of the object of the inner sense; in so far as all thinking, *i.e.*, we may take it, all consciousness, is only the accident of something, the real nature of which we have, therefore, no means of determining. Yet he had explicitly stated that the inner sense, which is altogether passive, has nothing to do with apperception, which is essentially active[4]. Apperception then is not a 'presented existence' (*ein Dasein*) an object 'posited,' but the activity of a subject, *ein Ichsein* as Fichte would

[1] Cf. above, p. 45 *n.* 2.

[2] Thereby, it is worth remarking by the way, only following in the footsteps of his rationalist forerunners, who failed even more completely to comprehend the nature of feeling.

[3] Hence *Dasein*, as we have seen, was one of Kant's categories.

[4] Cf. above, p. 153.

have said; and experience consists in its interaction with objects which are presented existences. The two are correlative, but they do not stand on a par. Nevertheless, Kant is continually attempting either to treat of them apart or to regard both as objects. *Together* (in experience) they cannot, however, both be objects alike given in sense —the subject merely an epiphenomenon (*Begleiterscheinung*) 'attached' or 'accompanying' the phenomena of external sense—for that, in so many words, is what Kant's inner sense comes to. *Apart*, on the other hand, they are but empty abstractions; and in that case, it is immaterial whether we designate them, like Locke, as 'a something we know not what,' or like Hume, as nothing that we know at all.

§ 25. *The Idea of Freedom*

But Kant in his second *Critique* treating of the Practical Reason had still more to say about the reality of the self. The main purpose of the first *Critique* had been to ascertain the limits of *Knowledge*, in order as he said to find a place for *Faith*. Accordingly, soon after completing the first edition of the *Critique of the Pure Reason*, he turned his attention to the problems of God, Freedom and Immortality, the three fundamental articles of his faith. Of these the Idea of Freedom was central. He came upon this Idea first in the second part of the *Dialectic*, dealing with cosmology. There an antithesis emerged between the understanding and reason concerning the causality implied in the world. In any series of events the understanding never gets beyond so-called 'causes' that are in turn effects of similar antecedent causes. Such endless chains of 'secondary or occasional causes,' each chain, so to say, 'hanging from nothing' does not satisfy reason, bent, as it is, on finding the 'Unconditioned.' So in the very dawn of philosophy the Idea arose of a First Cause, a prime mover, and generally, of causes that are not in turn effects. Such causes involve this Idea of Freedom. In Nature, however, we never come across causes of this sort, that is to say, 'primary or efficient causes.' Still, so long as we distinguish between phenomena and things *per se*, Freedom is at all events possible; but if phenomena were regarded as things *per se* it would be possible no longer. Further than this speculative reason cannot go.

For the practical reason, however, Freedom, as Kant said later[1], proves to be a fact. Of this fact we become aware through the 'categorical imperative' of reason (enacting unconditionally whatever is a duty); inasmuch as 'You ought' implies 'You can.' Freedom, then, is the *ratio essendi* of moral law, while moral law is the *ratio cognoscendi* of freedom[2]. Already in 1785, in his first ethical treatise, *Foundations of the Metaphysic of Morals*, Kant had got this far. In 1787, when the second edition of the first *Critique* was published, the *Critique of the Practical Reason* was on the point of being sent to the press, and actually appeared in the following year. Here Kant advances to his final position—the supremacy of the practical reason and with it an assured place for man as noumenal, a member of a supersensuous realm of ends. All this, however, though it was already present to his mind, Kant could as yet—in the context we have been considering—only indicate, but not fully expound (*vor-*

[1] Cf. above, pp. 129 f.
[2] *Kritik der praktischen Vernunft, Werke*, v. p. 4 *n.*, Abbott's trans. p. 88.

tragen): that belonged to the following *Critique*. So at the close of his discussion of the Idea of the Self from the standpoint of theoretical reason[1] we find him saying: "Let it be granted, however,...that certain *a priori* laws of reason should hereafter...turn out to occasion us to regard ourselves as legislating in respect of our own existence, ...in such wise that our *actuality (Wirklichkeit) was determinable* independently of the conditions of empirical intuition. We should then be immediately aware (*inne werden*) that there was something [more] included in the consciousness of our existence (*Dasein*), *viz.* a certain inner faculty capable of determining it—otherwise only sentiently determinable—in relation to an intelligible world....We should then be entitled to apply the categories of substance, cause, etc. in an *analogous* sense to freedom and to the subject that is free; though the ground for doing so is different from that of their logical use[2]."

But Kant is here putting the saddle on the wrong horse. It is not on the analogy of what we find that we interpret what we are. On the contrary it is the modes of the conscious self as knowing, feeling and willing, which are the source of the categories; and it is we who then apply these analogically to the Not-self which is there confronting us, and with which we interact. As Kant himself had just previously said, "in order to think them [the categories] it [the subject] must ground them on its [own] pure self-consciousness[3]." This truth then—the centrality of the experiencing subject—I think, we have

[1] His dissatisfaction with this he more than once admits. Cf. A. 387 *fin.*, Practical Reason, *Werke*, v. pp. 5 f. Abbott's trans. pp. 90 f.

[2] Cf. B. 430 f. (italics mine) and Erdmann, *Kants Kriticismus u.s.w.* pp. 223 f.

[3] B. 422.

reason for saying, comes out more and more clearly as we advance from Kant's first *Critique* of 1781 to the last in 1790, when he referred to his critical task as completed. In the first *Critique* this centrality is present as the transcendental unity of apperception and its '*creative synthesis*' as yielding formal and epistemological categories on which the possibility of all our systematic knowledge depends. In the second *Critique*, it is the self-determining, the *selective*, *activity* displayed in choice that is central, leading to axiological categories. In the third, it is feeling that bridges the gap between the other two by introducing aesthetic and teleological categories. Albeit we have to allow that Kant himself was not fully alive to all that his transcendental philosophy involved. It was left to others, notably to Fichte, to advance further into the promised land that he only dimly and partially descried.

It was Fichte who realised, as Kant never did, the importance of this knowing feeling and willing Self, round which nevertheless the whole of his critical philosophy turned. That Kant was the first philosopher who had '*thought*' this centrality of the self; that from Kant he, Fichte himself, had first learnt of it—of this much he was sure. But that Kant had not systematically *expounded* this supreme principle (*ein solches System aufgestelli*)—"this too," he added, "I know quite well"; for had Kant done so, his own epistemology (*Wissenschaftslehre*) would have been superfluous[1]. And here Fichte spoke only the simple truth, exemplifying, by the way, Kant's own saying, that another may often understand an author better than he understands himself. It was Fichte's merit again to proceed genetically, and Kant's defect to start from an archi-

---

[1] *Sämmtliche Werke*, 1845, I. p. 478.

tectonic of knowledge conceived as already complete[1]. So it was that Kant began, not with the primary factor in experience—the subject and its *functional* activity, but with certain disparate *forms* of knowledge, first those of sensibility, then those of understanding. Under the first head—in the *Aesthetic* he broached his transcendental idealism[2] with its pendant of an inner sense which, as we have seen, threatened to reduce the whole to an illusion, leaving scepticism or a baseless naturalism supreme. Under the second head—in the *Analytic*—he started *de novo*, but still proceeding in a more or less piecemeal fashion, the consequence of assuming sensibility and understanding to be disparate—the one purely passive the other entirely spontaneous. Yet he gets nearer to their 'possibly common root' in announcing the transcendental unity of *apperception* as 'the one,' and '*radical, faculty*[3].' Here the centrality of the subject in experience, the 'thought' with which Fichte credited him, emerges. Then, in passing to the second *Critique*, we come upon a further discontinuity, one between the practical reason, the topic of this and the theoretical reason, the topic of the first. Since, however, there is but one reason, it is essential to exhibit their unity in one common principle. So Kant expressed himself at the outset of his ethical inquiries[4] but without ever getting further than maintaining the *primacy* of the practical reason. But primacy so far from implying unity

[1] Cf. *Prolegomena*, Vorr. p. 21

[2] Though he did not give that name to it till much later.

[3] Cf. A. 114, 117 *n*. Thereby incidentally invalidating the doctrine of an inner sense, as we have, I believe, seen.

[4] *Werke*, iv. 239. Abbott's transl. p. 7. But when he came to write the second *Critique* he could still only 'expect that we may some day perhaps be able to discern this unity,' *Werke*, v. p. 95, Abbott's trans. p. 184.

involves duality at least; whilst in unity as such there is no order.

§ 26.   *Dualism of Theoretical and Practical Reason*

That this dualism of Kant's theoretical and practical reason is so far not transcended—is evident from the two voices in which they speak of freedom. Thus the theoretical reason declares freedom to be at most not a really impossible Idea[1], whilst the practical reason solemnly affirms it to be an awe-inspiring reality, since it entails duty in its train. Kant himself meanwhile—in his wonted rôle as mediator—seems to content himself with saying that it is a necessary postulate of moral conduct. Here, however, if—as Hegel said—we 'thoughtfully consider' experience broadly and as a whole, we find Kant again putting the saddle on the wrong horse. It is theory that needs a postulate and finds one, as he incidentally allowed[2]. Practice, on the other hand, like Bergson's *élan vital*, thrusts hither and thither 'canalising' a way as best it can; but with no postulate at all, only the impulse of self-conservation as a *vis a tergo* behind it. In short, experience as a whole is—as I have, perhaps, reiterated too often—just the process of becoming expert by experiment[3]. Kant as a man, knew this as well as any of us, but his inept conception of the philosophy of experience as an architectonic prevented him from working out his philosophy from the standpoint of experience as life. Had he done so, he would have begun his exposition of the primacy of the practical reason in the words in which he ended it: "all interest is

---

[1] A. 558 = B. 586.   [2] Cf. A. 735 ff. = B. 763 ff.
[3] Cf. *The Realm of Ends*, 3rd ed. 1920, pp. 412 ff.

ultimately practical; even that of speculative reason is only conditioned, and solely in the practical employment of reason is it complete[1]." But whereas Fichte (and Schopenhauer, who here only followed Fichte) took Kant's words in thorough earnest, Kant at this time failed to realise their full import completely. The dualism of theoretical and practical reason still remained; and, as we have seen, the gulf between them Kant did not succeed in bridging till he reached the problems of his final *Critique*.

It can, indeed, scarcely be said that anyone in the eighteenth century realised completely the wide range that many of us are now prepared to assign to Kant's words, "all interest is practical." It certainly cannot be said, if we except Leibniz whose *Monadology* appeared ten years before Kant was born. For Leibniz monads—all endowed with some activity—form a continuous series. Leaving aside questions concerning the extremes of the series— its upper and lower limits—we can say that the characteristics of any one monad within the series will differ from those of another in degree, but not in kind. Sense is thus continuous with understanding, and appetition with volition. Kant on the other hand set such continuity aside, regarding sense-knowledge and thought-knowledge—as we have already seen—as different in kind. And now in treating of freedom, he in like manner sharply differentiates between freedom and mere spontaneity. But as to any continuity between the two here also Kant has nothing to say[2]. So we come again upon the dualism between the

---

[1] *Werke*, v. p. 127, Abbott's trans. p. 218.

[2] Cf. *Werke*, v. pp. 101 f., 105; Abbott's trans. pp. 190 f., 195. But that differentiation is only justified if moral freedom is regarded as a species of spontaneity—spontaneity and something more. Neither here nor elsewhere has Kant seriously meant to accept the Cartesian doctrine of animal

phenomenal world of nature as a closed mechanical system and the noumenal world of things *per se*, or the realm of ends. And man, as amenable both to sensuous solicitation and to the call of duty, is thus a member of both worlds, is *homo phenomenon* and *homo noumenon* as well. His true vocation lies in the higher, but his probation begins in the lower, world.

Now we might understand this if only the continuity of the individual in these two 'characters' were clear: in other words, if the broad historical facts of development were in any way recognised. But in spite of his insistence on the limitation of our knowledge to experience, Kant seems here to make the continuity we naturally look for inconceivable, excluded from the outset by his doctrine of things *per se*; for as phenomenal, man is in time, as noumenal, he is not. And yet, if that were all, this difficulty might be met. Nay, more, the distinction of being in time or being out of time forecasts an important truth—if, that is to say, we distinguish (*a*) the time of the physicist, which is implicated with space and plotted out in a line, from (*b*) the living *durée*, as Bergson calls it, whence the real agents of the world spontaneously intervene, producing ever new events in 'the context of nature'—to use Kant's own phrase. There are sundry passages in his long discussion of the antinomy between nature and freedom which involve nothing beyond this distinction. Thus in exemplification of the thesis (maintaining the causality of freedom) he says: "If I now quite freely rise from my chair...then in this event together with its natural se-

automatism, to which he nevertheless unwarrantably alludes. Quite the contrary: cf. his distinction of kinds or grades of *Willkür*, below, p. 191, and above, pp. 115 f.

nizian monadology modified only by the substitution of
mutual interaction for pre-established harmony[1]. It was
announced dogmatically by Kant in his *Inaugural Dissertation*, and then thrown into the background in the
original edition of the first *Critique*, only gradually to re-
appear as 'the critical enterprise' advanced. But finally it
emerges again in the last *Critique*, in the doctrine of the
realm of ends, the consummation of that enterprise.

But Kant in expounding further the causality of freedom did not stop at that interpretation of *homo noumenon*
as "out of time" which we may allow to embody an
important truth; nor did he, in this connexion take due
account of that wider meaning of freedom as just initiative
or spontaneity of action. He is here concerned solely with
moral freedom, and this brings reason to the fore. Accordingly we soon find him talking not of the causality of the
individual as rational, but of causality in respect of
phenomena as a possible attribute of reason itself. Thus
causality out of time comes to be lined up with what
Spinoza meant by *sub specie aeternitatis*, where there is no
implication either of succession or of duration. So presently he speaks of reason as 'therefore, the constant
condition of all free (*willkürliche*) actions'; and this
causality of reason does *not arise* or begin at a certain
time; in it 'there is no *before or after*'; it is 'never in a new
state in which it was not before,' etc., etc.[2] Now there is a

---

[1] A monadology of this sort was upheld by Knutzen and adopted by
Kant from him. (Cf. B. Erdmann's *Martin Knutzen und seine Zeit* (1875),
pp. 65 and ch. iv.) As to Kant's private monadological opinions, cf. the
same writers, *Kants Kriticismus*, pp. 73 ff. and 223 ff., and for further
details, a dissertation by a pupil of his, O. Riedel, entitled *Die monadolo-
gischen Bestimmungen in Kants Lehre vom Ding an sich*, 1884.

[2] Cf. A. 549–56 = B. 579–84 *passim*.

sense in which we can understand even this language; it is appropriate in symbolic logic or in the theory of numbers, for example; but it is quite out of place in the discussion of the problem of cosmology in which these passages occur. That problem is one concerning agents, and though Spinoza talked of *ratio sive causa*, Kant had barred out any such equivocation long ago[1]. Here, however, he seems to be getting near to the rationalist confusion of reason and cause. Moreover, so long as the broad question concerned the existence at all of initiating agents, who intervene in the 'course of nature' phenomenally regarded, its restriction to only one class of such agents could not be justified. But Kant also refers to the reason as 'having causality in respect of its objects' when he comes to treat of the practical reason[2]. However, as the whole context shews, the actual agent is now the *homo noumenon*, and all that reason does is to provide him with a *motive*: though it may 'command,' it cannot constrain.

§ 27. *The Concrete Individual*

'The reason' and 'the *homo noumenon*,' however, are here general terms and so far do not denote a concrete individual. Thus it was possible for Kant to get both under one hat, if such a vulgar expression may be allowed. Thereby he is enabled to bring the practical reason into 'the good company of mathematics' as he believed long before that he had brought the theoretical reason[3]. Hence

[1] Cf. above, pp. 18 f.
[2] *Grundlegung zur Metaphysik der Sitten, Werke,* iv. p. 296, Abbott's trans. p. 67.
[3] Cf. above, p. 77.

the severely formal character of his categorical imperative[1]. But difficulties arise as soon as we pass from these abstractions to individual men and their deliberate actions. Kant surprises us here with a remark which shews again how completely he neglected the historical side of experience. To explain in a particular case "why the intelligible character should...give these phenomena and this empirical character and no other, this," he says, "as much transcends all [the] power of our reason...as if we were to ask whence the transcendental object of our external intuition gives [us] intuition in *space* only and no other at all[2]." We need hardly waste time commenting on the complete lack of correspondence between particular cases no two of which are alike, and a case in which all are alike inasmuch as they all wear space-spectacles. But there are two questions that we must consider.

First, what after all in the case of a concrete individual is the relation of his intelligible to his sensible character? So far Kant has regarded the latter as wholly phenomenal and thus separated from the former by the theoretically impassable boundary between phenomena and things *per*

---

[1] Cf. *Kritik d. prakt. Vern.*, pref. p. 8 *n.*, Abbott's trans. p. 93 "Whoever knows of what importance to a mathematician a *formula* is which accurately defines what is to be done to work out a problem without fail will note that a formula which does the same for all duty whatever is unimportant and superfluous." Again in contrasting the 'simplicity' of the moral with these manifold requirements of duty which can be drawn from it, he confesses there to 'mathematical postulates as being *indemonstrable* and yet apodeictic.' *Met. d. Sitten*, p. 22 *fin.*, Abbott's transl. p. 281 *fin.*

It would be interesting to know whether Kant was aware that Locke also "had made bold to think that morality is capable of demonstration as well as mathematics"; or whether he knew anything of the views of Samuel Clarke or Cumberland.

[2] A. p. 557 = B. p. 585.

se. But this boundary is already passed when the two are connected as real cause and phenomenal effect. The sensible character, however, as phenomenal and so a part of the 'context of nature,' cannot be distinguished as the effect of the intelligible character exclusively. We have, as Kant himself points out, no means of unravelling the phenomenal tissue to that extent[1]. The two characters then, it would seem, can not only not be clearly distinguished, but it cannot be straightway assumed that they are really distinct. But here we must recall what has been already incidentally noticed: the sensible character, in so far as it pertains to a real agent, cannot be accounted a part of nature as a closed system, cannot, in short be explained on mechanical lines, as Kant fully recognised in the teleological part of his last *Critique*[2]. All things living intervene to modify what would have been the course of nature left to itself. Admitting this we are at the historical standpoint. We can no longer ignore the fact that the individual manifests what Kant calls a sensible character before there is either for it or others any clear evidence that it possesses an intelligible one.

So we come to our second question: How has this advance come about; how has the individual come to participate in that eternal reason, regarded by Kant too much as a thing apart; how has he come to find himself potentially autonomous as a member of a realm of ends? This is the converse of the question which Kant pronounced insoluble, owing to the discontinuity of his way of approach. Approached from the historical side the answer is simple enough and Kant has given it a name, if

---

[1] Cf. A. 549 *fin.* = B. 587 *fin.*; A. 551 *m.* = B. 579 *m.*

[2] Cf. above, pp. 125 f.

I rightly understand him: it is *Bewusstsein überhaupt,* the common consciousness of the self-conscious. As Fichte said, Kant had the thought, but he nowhere attempted systematically to unfold it. It is, in fact, involved in his transcendental unity of apperception, which he supposed he had ascertained by simply—like Locke—'looking into his own mind[1].' Self-consciousness and the vastly wider horizon that it eventually discloses are the result of inter-subjective intercourse; and the knowledge which Kant called transcendental is psychologically trans-subjective. Kant shared in what Caird has called 'the individualism of the eighteenth century.' Much as Leibniz's monad developed as if there were nothing in existence save itself and God, so the individual seems to develope according to Kant. *Entre l'homme et la nature il faut l'humanité*—this great saying of Auguste Comte conveys a truth to which Immanuel Kant was blind. Though he talked of epi-genesis he thought only of preformation. As we cannot, he supposed, get behind the fact that our external per-ception is spatial, so—in regard to human volition—"we can get only so far as the intelligible cause but not beyond[2]." "Get so far," forsooth, but Kant did not *get* so far: it was with reason as 'intelligible cause' that he started, and now he cannot get back from there to where we are historically. Here it is that we find the primacy of 'practice' on which Kant insisted; but it is not in its beginning practical *reason*, but simply the *conatus* of Spinoza—'the impulse to self-conservation and better-ment.' So as the race and the individual progress, the 'motives' change, and with intersubjective intercourse, reason and conscience emerge at length. All this is now

---

[1] Cf. p. 58 above.   [2] A. 557 *init.* = B. 585 *init.*

historical commonplace; but it was beyond the scope of Kant's first *Critique* and only very partially realised in the second[1].

§ 28. Religion within the bounds of mere reason

In 1793, three years after he had declared his critical labours completed, Kant produced the last important work which the student of his philosophy need consider. It is entitled *Religion within the Bounds of Mere Reason*. This title seems at first sight perplexing; for in the first *Critique* he had so determined the bounds of pure specu- lative reason, that nothing can there be *posited* concerning religion at all; and in the second *Critique*, he claimed to shew that the pure practical reason *postulates* all that is essential as the basis of religious faith. What more then can there be for 'mere reason' to say? However in the work itself we find that it is not a philosophy of religion in general, but chiefly an examination of the connexion between 'natural religion,' as Hume called it, and religion as 'revealed' in the New Testament. Kant has given several descriptions of religion; but he has nowhere attempted an adequate definition of it as a factor in human experience[2]. It is historically certain that the religious

[1] I have tried to treat of it more than once elsewhere, and may here perhaps refer to *Naturalism and Agnosticism*, 4th ed. (1915), pp. 481 ff., earlier edns. ii. pp. 189 ff.

[2] Perhaps the nearest approach to one is that given in the present work: "All religion consists in this, that we look upon God as (the Being) to be universally worshipped (*verehrenden*) as the Lawgiver of all our duties" (*Religion innerhalb die Grenzen u.s.w.*, *Werke*, vi. p. 201). With this the following may be compared: "Religion—as contrasted with Paganism—is the faith which puts (*setzt*) the *essential* of all worship of God in the moral nature of man." *Conflict of the Faculties, Werke*, vii. p. 366.

consciousness does not arise from conscience alone. In its higher forms it may be described as 'morality touched with emotion'; but the emotion precedes the morality, either as wonder, fear, hope, or all combined. But this aspect of religion, Kant—owing to his strong rationalistic bias and lack of historical sense—entirely ignores[1].

The greater part of the present work, in fact, is devoted to a well-meant endeavour to find a rational justification of the dogmas, ordinances and institutions of the 'visible church' of Christendom. Here, no doubt, his inbred 'pietism' breaks out. The sad declension of this church from its ethical ideal, the confusion of true 'divine service' with ritual observances, and the '*saying* of prayers'— which he compared with the prayer mills of Thibet—he exposes as unflinchingly as a Hebrew prophet: all such matters at all events are outside the bounds of reason; and he insists on the right of reason to 'protest,' and refuses to surrender this right to any authority. For so doing he received a threatening reprimand from the servile and hypocritical Minister of Education, who, on the death of Frederick the Great, had succeeded his old patron, von Zedlitz. Though deserving of mention as shewing Kant in a new light and also as an important episode in his life, it would be out of place to enlarge on this here. All we need now consider is Kant's handling of two fundamental dogmas of the Christian creed—Original Sin and the New Birth.

[1] If we except very incidental reference in connexion with the Sublime in § 29 and with Morality in § 59 of the *Critique of Judgment*.

§ 29. *Man's native Capacities*

Here the only philosophical problem raised is still concerned with freedom, the problem we have just been discussing. But the atmosphere, so to say, of the discussion is changed. Not rational will (*Wille*) but arbitrary will (*Willkür*) is now the fundamental idea: the standpoint, in other words, is more psychological. Moreover the bounds imposed on reason in the first *Critique* seem here to be disregarded: Kant is again dogmatic.

First of all then the terminology used calls for some attention. To begin, it is to be remarked that the phrase 'human nature' is used in two senses. It is sometimes the actual nature that man has acquired by the use of his freedom, sometimes the potential nature with which he is endowed. On the practical side, the capacity for the Good (*Anlage zum Guten*) of human nature in the latter sense, this Kant divides into (1) the capacity for *animality*, *i.e.* as living; (2) the capacity for *humanity*, as living and rational; (3) the capacity for *personality*, as rational and responsible[1]. To each of these capacities there is an appropriate form of *Willkür*: (1) an *arbitrium brutum*, determinable by sensory impulse; (2) an *arbitrium sensitivum*, not *brutum*, as it is only affected but not determined by sense, and so far an *arbitrium liberum*, although not pure; (3) what Kant might have called *arbitrium rationale*: it is *liberum arbitrium*, in the positive sense, the will (*Wille*) of pure practical

[1] *Op. cit.* p. 120, Abbott's trans. p. 332 (where by some mischance in the title *Anlage* is translated *Incapacity*!). The correspondence between this division with Butler's blind propensions, self-love, and conscience is striking; for, as Abbott has pointed out, Kant, like Germans generally, seems to have known nothing of Butler. Cf. his *Kant's Theory of Ethics*, 6th ed. (1909), p. lxii.

reason[1]. In place of affection by sense, the capacity for personality is the susceptibility of respect (*Achtung*) for the moral law *as in itself an adequate spring of action of the arbitrary will*[2]. Now such a spring the law cannot be, unless the free (*i.e.* the rational) will adopt the law as its maxim. Then, however, he adds, the idea of the moral law with the respect inseparable from it cannot well be called a *capacity* for *personality*: it is the idea of personality itself (the idea of humanity considered entirely [as] intellectual). Yet even so, as merely persons, we still have an *Anlage*, *i.e.* a subjective ground, additional to personality, for adopting [or not adopting] the moral law into our maxims. It is on this that moral character depends.

Though Kant makes reason an 'element' both of humanity and personality, he is careful to point out that its meaning is very different in the two cases. The former —for which he might easily have found a better word— is simply intelligence, the capacity by forethought for the morrow to secure and promote the ends of prudent self-love[3]. No extension of so-called reason of this sort would ever enable us to discover the moral law, if this law 'were not given in us.' But it may be objected: has not Kant maintained that in respect of this law we are autonomous? That, however, only implies that the law is not given *to* us, in other words is not by nature imposed on us. To say, then, that the law is given in us is only to say that we are

---

[1] These details, however, are given elsewhere. Cf. *Metaphysik der Sitten*, *Werke*, vii. p. 10, Abbott's trans. p. 268, and *Critique*, A. 534 = B. 562.

[2] P. 121, Abbott, p. 334. As to the difference between this esteem and passive 'feelings' cf. *Grundlegung u.s.w.*, *Werke*, iv. 249 *n*. Abbott's trans. p. 17 *n*.

[3] Cf. *Anthropologie*, *Werke*, vii. 39, 46.

not merely intelligent beings but are conscious that we
are also responsible beings. So far good. But under what
circumstances are we aware of such personal responsibility? When we realise that we live in and interact with
a world that—for us—is not merely a natural world but
a social or civil world as well—ideally a spiritual world, a
realm of ends. This fact Kant recognised indeed and
directly connected the moral law with such a realm; but
in consequence of his adherence to the individualistic
standpoint he has inverted the order of the two[1].

This brings us to the relation of two of Kant's terms
which here becomes clear, *viz.* Maxim and Law. A maxim
is simply a rule adopted by the individual in the pursuit
of his own ends as dictated by self-love. The moral law,
on the other hand, holds universally for the realm of ends;
and it is in acknowledging fealty to this that the individual
becomes enfranchised as a member of that invisible realm.
And whoever is not 'with it is against it'; for neutrality
is impossible here: in short he who is not good is bad.
This moral attitude Kant speaks of as *Gesinnung*, meaning
'the subjective ground' referred to above[2], regarded as a
disposition rather than merely a deed. But now we are
brought up against difficulties. We can conceive a man,
who has voluntarily adopted a maxim, to persevere in
acting in accordance with it and, so acquiring a disposi-

[1] Cf. *Grundlegung, Werke*, IV. pp. 281 f. Abbott's trans. pp. 51 f.

[2] Some remark on this term seems called for. A glance at a German
dictionary will shew that it has no single and precise equivalent in English.
Its commonest meaning, sentiment, is obviously inappropriate here: Kant
often calls that *Sinnesart*. 'Mindedness' as in noble-mindedness, base-
mindedness (*edle, niedrige, Gesinnung*) comes nearer; and so Kant often
calls *Gesinnung* in this sense *Denkungsart*; but we have no such general
term. Anyhow a permanent state, not a single act, is connoted: 'disposition,'
the rendering given by Dr Abbott, at least expresses this and so is used here.

tion. In keeping with this Kant himself had already remarked that "in good dispositions, and not in actions
only, consists the high worth which humanity can and
ought thereby to acquire[1]." To acquire, yes; but can we
say that a man can start by voluntarily adopting a disposition? Yet Kant does say this. Further, "since we
cannot derive this disposition...from any first act of
arbitrary will (*Willkür*) we therefore," he says, "call it a
quality (*Beschaffenheit*) of this pertaining to it by nature
(although, in fact, grounded on freedom)." Clearly by
nature here the second nature which is acquired is meant,
not the nature which consists entirely of capacities
(*Anlagen*). So, to say that a man has one or other disposition as an 'innate natural quality' does not mean, Kant
expressly tells us, "that it is not acquired by him but only
that it is not acquired in time[2]."

In his exposition of human nature in the first sense
Kant made no mention of either adopting or acquiring
dispositions at all. But in reference to the two lower
capacities, animality and humanity, he spoke of the possibility of *grafting* on these, vices which do not spring of
themselves from nature as their root. Even as regards
personality, as we have already seen, nothing is said of
acquiring or even adopting a disposition till the capacity
is actualized, and then we have the subjective ground of
free will which converts personality into character by
accepting or rejecting the moral law. Now on this capacity,
Kant declares, "*nothing evil can be grafted*." We might
understand that a rational being, who elected for evil,

---

[1] *Werke*, v. p. 75, Abbott's trans. p. 163, where, however, *Gesinnun-
gen* is translated 'intentions.'
[2] P. 119, Abbott, p. 332.

might—loosely speaking—be said itself to graft on the lower capacities vices which could never spring from mere animality or from humanity, regarded as just the attribute of an individual. Even so the analogy of grafting, which implies external interference, is anything but apposite; inasmuch as it is incompatible with the unity and continuity of the individual. But we should not expect Kant with his sharp distinction between the phenomenal and the noumenal, to be awake to this defect in his analogy: assuming, then, that we are entitled to talk of a noumenal *Anlage* at all, it is not clear why this one *Anlage* shall be an exception. In one respect, in Kant's view it is not. All our natural capacities are liable to be 'abused' or perverted (*verdirbt*), but none can be eradicated (*vertilgt*). This one alone, however, can not only not be eradicated, it cannot even be perverted[1]. Unfortunately we shall find that Kant never defines precisely what this *Anlage* is. So far he has described personality as constituted by the possession of the idea of the moral law and the feeling of respect or reverence which is inseparable from that idea. But what he affirms to be incorruptible is simply the practical reason, which categorically enounces the law as a command. It is impossible to think that reason itself should eradicate respect for its own law and repudiate the responsibility which that entails. Such malignant practical reason (an absolutely bad will) would be devilish, and that epithet is not applicable to humanity[2]. And later on, in treating of Regeneration we find Kant saying: "It must be presupposed indeed, that in humanity *a germ of the good has persisted through all in its entire purity* and this [germ] can

---

[1] Cf. p. 139, Abbott's trans. p. 353.
[2] P. 129, Abbott, p. 342.

certainly not be self-love, which, when taken as the principle of all our maxims, is the source of all evil[1]."

§ 30. *Human Nature as radically bad*

So we come to Kant's rational interpretation of the doctrine of Original Sin as it is said to be revealed. Here, in spite of all that we have just found him saying, he maintains that Man is *by nature radically bad*. Since he held that Man "was created for good and that his original constitution is good," this, it would seem, can only mean that Man has made himself bad, freely elected so to be. In that case, however, would he not after all have become a devil? As we may expect, it will turn out that Kant does not mean what he seems to say. However let us first follow his exposition.

This, like the exposition of the original capacity for good in human nature, is in the main psychological. It introduces, however, a new term, *viz.* propensity (*Hang*). This differs from an original capacity (*Anlage*) in being contingent, not essential, to human nature as such. It is defined as "properly only the predisposition to the desire of an enjoyment which—when *the subject has had experience of it*—brings forth an inclination (*Neigung*) to it." By way of illustration Kant refers to savages who, as altogether unacquainted with intoxication, can have no craving for alcohol until they have tasted it; but once they have done so, acquire a craving for it that is hardly to be eradicated. "But now," Kant remarks, "it is only the propensity to the morally-bad that is in question[2]." May we not ask then whether what is morally bad, once

[1] P. 139. Italics mine.   [2] Pp. 122 f., Abbott, p. 335.

its results are experienced, can be conceived as begetting an insatiable desire for it? The savage, however, tastes in ignorance, *i.e.* innocently; whereas moral badness, as Kant goes on to recall, is possible only as the deliberate resolve, or—as he presently adds—as the deed of a responsible person, responsible because free either to accept or to reject the moral law. But why must such a deed involve a *predisposition* of any sort—a *peccatum in potentia*, of which Kant talks, any more than a *sanctitas in potentia*, as to which he says nothing? To talk of a predisposition here is only to push back the question *ad indefinitum* without making any advance. For any predisposition that involves responsibility leaves us where we were before, and one that does not puts an end to responsibility altogether. This much Kant himself at the very outset of the discussion pointed out as obvious, and accordingly, then and often afterwards, declared the whole question to be insoluble[1].

Insoluble on such lines, we have, I think, already found this problem to be. Yet it may be otherwise if we approach it historically, that is to say empirically and genetically. And we shall find Kant himself soon sliding over on to these lines. So much so, that it is uncertain in the transition in which of his two senses he is using the term nature. Thus he began by stating that "if this propensity may be assumed as belonging to Man universally (and so to the character of his race) [it] is to be called a *natural* propensity to evil." But the only adequate justification for assuming such universality must, on Kantian principles, be *a priori*, and then universality implies necessity[2].

[1] Cf. p. 115*n*. Abbott, p. 328.
[2] P. 123, Abbott, p. 336. As he is fond on occasion of appealing to Scripture what would Kant have said of Seth and perhaps of Elijah?

Again he remarks, "this propensity to evil...is here ascribed even to the best of men..., and it must be so ascribed, if the universality of the propensity to evil in Man is to be proved (*bewiesen*), in other words, that it is interwoven (*verwebt*) with human nature[1]." Meanwhile the said assumption involves Kant in something like an antinomy[2]. Briefly put the thesis is: This propensity, being morally bad and not a natural capacity, must, on account of freedom, be regarded as *contingent*. The antithesis is: But such contingency is *inconsistent* with the universality of the badness. The solution he offers is the only proof of the assumption that he seems ever to give. It is this: "The ultimate subjective ground of all maxims, be it by what means it may, is interwoven with humanity itself, and so to say, rooted in it." This ground, that is to say, is an original capacity of humanity and so universal; but that is not bad. So far the antithesis seems right. Kant, however, continues: "Hence we can call this [propensity] a natural propensity to evil." This is nature in the second sense, the universality of which is to be proved. But how can propensity be inferred from capacity, if it is not essentially involved in it? He then concludes: "Since it[3] [the propensity] *must* nevertheless always be self-incurred (*selbstverschuldet*) [we can call it] a radical, innate badness (*Böse*) in human nature but none the less 'put on' by ourselves." But here the 'putting on' of the 'natural man' (with the guilt thereby incurred) is too obviously regarded as a personal deed (*That*) to justify any assumption of its uni-

---

[1] P. 124, Abbott, p. 337 *init.*
[2] Cf. p. 126, Abbott, p. 339 (italics mine).
[3] Abbott translates *er* as referring to *Mensch*, not to *Hang*, but the *ihn* that immediately follows certainly refers to *Hang*.

versality in the race on Kantian lines, *i.e.* as what he calls
"*peccatum originarium*...an intelligible deed only cognis-
able by reason, apart from any condition of time." If
however it is only what he calls '*peccatum derivativum, i.e.*
sensible, empirical, given in time (*factum phenomenon*),'
then it cannot so far be radical in the strict sense[1]—that
would mean being devilish, as Kant has already allowed.

How far Kant intended this passage even to suggest an
a priori proof of the radical badness of human nature is
questionable. But what interests us here is the sentence
which immediately follows. It is this: "Now that such a
corrupt propensity must be rooted in human nature—as
to that we may spare [ourselves] the formal proof, in view
of the multitude of crying examples which experience of
the deeds of men puts before our eyes." He proceeds to
cite instances from the bloodthirstiness of Red Indians
and South Sea islanders to the cynicism of Sir Robert
Walpole. Presently, however, he breaks off with the remark, that though the existence of this evil propensity
can be shewn from experience, yet this does not teach us

[1] Cf. pp. 125 f.; Abbott, pp. 337 f. In this long paragraph Kant admits
that there would be a contradiction in the concept of a mere propensity to
evil "unless the expression 'deed' (*That*) could be taken in two different
senses, both of which, however, are compatible with freedom—(1) that
use of freedom whereby one's supreme maxim (for or against the moral
law) is *adopted* (*aufgenommen*), (2) that in which actions (*Handlungen*) are
performed (*ausgeübt*) in conformity with it. Fortified with this distinction
he thinks he was entitled to say that a propensity "is a subjective ground of
arbitrary will (*Willkür*) which *precedes every deed*, and is therefore itself
not yet a deed." At the end of the paragraph we find him saying: "Why
in us the Evil (*das Böse*) has corrupted the supreme maxim, although this
is our own deed; for this we can as little assign a cause beyond it as [we
can] for any other (*einer*) fundamental attribute belonging to our nature."
What do 'the Evil' and 'our nature' mean here? Are they distinct or not?
Either way Kant seems in difficulties.

[what is] its intrinsic nature (*eigentliche Beschaffenheit*):
this must be cognized *a priori* from the concept of the
Bad. He then proceeds to expound 'the development of
that concept.' It is difficult to find what there is that is
a priori about this; but underlying it we readily discern
its resemblance to the avowedly empirical accounts of the
development of our moral nature, which Kant might have
found in his contemporaries, Butler and Adam Smith,
had he known of them.

First of all we note the statement that man by nature
depends on (*hängt an*) sensory impulses[1]. In saying this
Kant is contemplating Man as connected with the phenomenal world, not as acting in it but as 'stimulated' by
it, Man regarded at the animal level, all the will he has
being just *arbitrium brutum*. The development, which
Kant is undertaking to expound *a priori*, begins then in
time, where 'before and after' are vital, not out of time
where they are supposed to be meaningless. Yet he
assumes—most inconsistently surely—that Man is already
in possession both of an *arbitrium sensitivum* and an
arbitrium liberum or rational will. Accordingly, at the *very*
outset he conceives Man as *naturally* (*natürlicher Weise*)
amenable to motives of two kinds, those which his
individual intelligence suffices to supply—motives dictated
by self-love—as well as motives which only conscience
can dictate. So he then concludes: "The distinction,
whether a man is good or bad, must lie not in the distinction of his motives, but in the *subordination* [of them]:
which of the two he makes the condition of the other[2]." Well,

---

[1] Here there is a '*Hang*' that is more than a propensity, but it is declared
to be 'guiltless.'

[2] P. 130, Abbott, p. 343.

Man inverts the moral order and rates the second first. But why? Starting from the noumenal, and ignoring the phenomenal, side, Kant—as we have already more than once seen—found this a question which admits of no answer. Now, however, he gives one. "Man, realising that the said motives cannot subsist together, but that one must be subordinated to the other as its supreme condition, makes the motives arising from self-love and its inclinations the condition of obedience to the moral law[1]." But he goes further still. Regardless of the fact that he is dealing with a development in time, that he had already recognised a gradation of capacities, and that, moreover, he had distinguished between reason as mere intelligence and the practical reason which enounces the moral law— he now makes an assumption contrary to all this as well as to all that we empirically know. Reason in the former sense, he now supposes, "may employ the unity of maxims in general, which is proper to the moral law, merely to introduce into the motives arising from inclination a unity, under the name of *happiness*, that cannot otherwise accrue to them. If now," he continues, "there is in human nature a propensity to this [that is, I take it, to seek happiness first] then..."—in short human nature is radically bad[2].

But unless self-love were there, unless happiness were desired before morality is possible, how should we ever have got any further? If there must be social intercourse and intelligence before *any* law can be framed, how in the order of development can the immutable moral law have been recognised first? And finally—a very damaging consideration—since Kant postulated the existence of God in

[1] P. 130, Abbott, p. 343.   [2] P. 131, Abbott, p. 344.

order that eventually happiness should be proportional to virtue, what meaning is there in a purely formal law, *unless* the Idea of the Good, which implies happiness as well as virtue, is after all supreme? As Lotze urged, what sense is there in a purely formal law if, as Kant maintained, it has no object beyond itself?

Finally, in this very section Kant goes on immediately to say that Man has only "a bad heart...which may subsist with a will good in general," and in the next proceeds to shew that accordingly his moral regeneration is possible. To say nothing of clouding the issue by this reference to a vague Scriptural phrase, we come here upon a fundamental antinomy or perhaps it were truer to say a characteristic vacillation in Kant when faced with final problems. If human nature is verily radically bad there can be no regeneration, yet Kant has seemed to maintain that both are true, even throwing back the badness into the noumenal which is out of time.

*   *   *   *   *

The general summary which would have been appropriate here is reserved for the lecture referred to in the preface. This is to appear in the *Proceedings of the British Academy* for the present year.

INDEX

Self-love, 191 *n.*, 200, 201
Self, Idea of, 90 f., 151 *n.*, 156 ff., 176; not an object, 159 (see also Subject)
Sense-data (= 'sense manifold'), 53
Sensible, the, and intelligible different in kind for Kant, 29; and this divides him from Leibniz, 38
Sin, 197 ff.
SMITH, ADAM, 200
Space, Kant's views on, 7; difference of regions in, 34 f.
Specification, law of, 96 ff.
Subject, 49 f., 82, 155
Sufficient Reason, 9 f.; and Cause, 11
Synthesis, apperceptive, 49; grades of S., 150 *n.*; figural S., 153; categorial S., 154
Synthetic Judgment, supreme principle of, 65 ff.

Teleology, and mechanism, 8; principle of, 121–4; not constitutive for K., 122 f.; the idea for, prescribed by reason, 125–8; and theology, 128–31
Thing, Things, *per se*, 51; as causes, 53, 183

Transcendental, why K. so entitled his philosophy, 50; what remains of it, 79 ff.; its central truth, 80; this the direct source of real categories, 81 f.; transcendental subject and transcendental object as correlative, 82; the primary importance of movement, overlooked by K., confirms this correlation, 83 f.; yet K. failed to hold fast to his central fact, 84 f.; things *per se* as unknown X or X's threaten to reduce experience to illusion, 85; the relation of subject and object not symmetrical, 86; positive selection confined to the former, 86

Understanding, its fundamental principles, 60 ff.; distinction of, as constitutive and regulative, 64; as the law-giver to Nature, 61

Will, grades of, 191
WOLFF, CASPAR, upholder of epigenesis, 55
WOLFF, CHR., as systematizer of Leibniz, 9; made the principle of contradiction the basis of philosophy, 9

CAMBRIDGE: PRINTED BY J. B. PEACE, M.A., AT THE UNIVERSITY PRESS